ST. JOSEPH'S COLLEGE OF EDUCATION LIBRARY

This book is issued in accordance with current College
Library Regulations.

DATE DUE AT LIBRARY LAST STAMPED BELOW

Social Anthropology

Social Anthropology

David F. Pocock

*Dean of the School of African and Asian Studies
in the University of Sussex*

Sheed and Ward · London and Sydney

First published 1961 under the auspices of
the Newman Association of Great Britain
Second revised edition 1971
Sheed and Ward Ltd,
33 Maiden Lane, London WC2E 7LA
and
Sheed and Ward Pty Ltd,
204 Clarence Street, Sydney NSW 2000
© David F. Pocock 1971

SBN 7220 0626 8

This book is set in 11 pt Monotype Baskerville
Made and printed by offset in Great Britain by
William Clowes and Sons, Limited
London, Beccles and Colchester

For

G.M.P.
L.C.P.

PREFACE TO THE SECOND EDITION

This book first appeared ten years ago and is now being re-issued, minor corrections aside, in its original form. Had I re-written it my first intention would have been to amplify some of its more compressed passages but I could not then have resisted the temptation to re-distribute the emphases and, in short, would finally have found myself writing an entirely new account and producing a piece of work quite different in nature from the original.

The circumstances in which my *Social Anthropology* was published, for the Newman Philosophy of Science Series, the very brevity required, enabled me to be more idiosyncratic than I could have been had I been required to write a text-book intended to be authoritative. My intention while writing was, then, to carry out a sort of personal stock-taking and to express what was authoritative for me if not for anyone else. I make this point because I have been chidden by a colleague for passing off a selected intellectual genealogy as a "history of the subject".[1] Because I used a historical mode I was not, for all that, setting out to write a history. I was writing very much as a traditional genealogist in India constructs a genealogy for his client according to his present circumstances. Any anthropologist in India or,

I suppose, in Africa will know how a sudden change in the political or economic circumstances of some segment of a caste or tribe brings into prominence an ancestor hitherto undistinguished or even neglected. The notion that I had essayed a "history of the subject" has occurred elsewhere and I therefore take this opportunity to disclaim such grand pretensions. The book is then a personal account but, evidently, it contains assumptions which I shared with my colleagues at Oxford at that time, together with the common debt which we all owed to Professor Evans-Pritchard.

So long as weighty correctives are available to the student an idiosyncratic view can be useful if it reminds him of the inescapably personal quality of his own anthropology. He comes to the subject with an anthropology ready formed by virtue of his being social—a mass of myths, concepts, judgements of value and reality, expectations and the like. One of the first, certainly one of the most important, duties of his tutor is to help him to see that this is so and to encourage him to examine the nature of this, still largely inarticulate, private social world. It is because he is conscious of his personal anthropology that he can make it interact with the formal anthropologies of his discipline. He becomes an anthropologist not by sacrificing his personal anthropology to any "official view" nor by the romantic assertion of his individuality but by developing the capacity to put the two in a permanent relation. It is probably true of all students of the social sciences that unless they become conscious of what I have called their personal anthropologies they run the risk of reinforcing a split between the "received ideas" and their private sense of the matter; they are all set, in other words, for the posture of "alienation".

As an academic discipline for the undergraduate, and for many the last formal education they will receive, anthropology has various moral and intellectual values but I am convinced that its greatest value is realised where it helps the student to develop a sociological sensibility, an anthropological consciousness which has nothing to do with intellectual agility or brilliance. The students of Marcel Mauss discovered that he added a new dimension to their existence and when academic anthropology achieves this for any individual it has been educative in the literal and in the best sense of the word.

This emphasis upon a personal anthropology derives as much from an intellectual concern as from a moral one. The growth of anthropology in this country as an academic discipline involves the risk of that kind of petrification which can occur when an enquiry originally undertaken by adult individuals becomes a "subject" to be taught to the young and is reduced to "text-books", set courses and select bibliographies. If the student "does" anthropology then, whatever he himself may acquire in the way of agility, it is the subject itself

which is done for. Evidently there are some
university "subjects" such as, one is led to
understand, classics, which do not suffer this
kind of brutalisation but if anthropology is not
lived at the same time as it is learned it will
reduce itself to a set of dubious propositions
about a set of societies which have long since
ceased to exist. The danger of such a fossiliza-
tion is heightened as on the one hand student
numbers increase and access to the supposedly
privileged areas of anthropological enquiry is
reduced by qualitative and quantitative change.

What is true for the individual student is true
for the discipline as it evolves in any particular
society. Although anthropology emerged first
in the western world it is now firmly established in India, for example, and is at least
being rapidly fed into the Japanese consciousness through several translations. If it is
proffered and approached as a finished object,
if it is taken in as something to be learned, there
is a grave danger that it could be uncritically
accepted as a part of the package called
"westernisation" to float upon the receiving
consciousness unmodified and as unmodifiable
as a plastic bucket taken from the same source.
There is in India, as I don't doubt in other
parts of the world, a kind of intellectual bi-
lingualism among some academics which effectively and affectively cuts off the chosen
specialisation from the rest of life. This is,
apparently, by no means crippling for the
mathematician or the physicist but for a

practitioner of social science it is utterly stultifying. Indian anthropology must be truly Indian in the first place and not, necessarily, ask the questions which foreign anthropologists have asked, according to *their* intellectual needs, of Indian society.

I should make it clear that I am not saying that an Indian, or a Japanese anthropology for that matter, would be a separate let alone isolated anthropology but it would be one that emerged in the first instance from the consciousness of being Indian or being Japanese and develop by interacting with and so contributing to other anthropologies in the world. It is easy to see that a universal anthropology could only be the product of a world society. If this view that there are national or local anthropologies is doubted I would refer the reader to a recent publication by Professor Marvin Harris of Columbia University and particularly to his account of British social anthropology. At the same time the anthropology of Claude Lévi-Strauss, which was born out of French, British and American anthropologies, exemplifies the possibility of interaction and synthesis. Because this second edition coincides with the appearance of the Japanese translation I express here the hope that it will assist to provoke Japanese thought about Japanese society and that its very idiosyncrasy will preclude its being accepted as authoritative.

This book is then the view of a British social

anthropologist at Oxford in 1960 and the reader will note a rather exclusive and, he may think, even parochial tone. This is itself significant. Professor Lévi-Strauss has rebuked me privately for the rather ludicrous passing reference to Franz Boas, whom Marvin Harris regards as of "central importance in the establishment of the discipline".[2] My remark now certainly seems absurd (below, p. 47). Nevertheless at the time that I was writing Boas and his school who, I admit, provided the only introductory "text-books" for my own student generation, had passed almost completely out of contemporary view.

A more serious gap but one which can be accounted for in much the same way is the complete lack of reference to the work of Max Weber for all that the influence of German thought on developments in America was noted (below, p. 66). Although Weber was known, chiefly for his *Protestant Ethic and the Spirit of Capitalism*, and even admired by some, his thought and the problems which he raised did not flow into the main stream. Talcott Parsons had spelt out Weber's importance in English in 1937 as had Raymond Aron a year earlier in his *La Sociologie Allemande Contemporaine* where he describes Weber's work as marking "an epoch in the history of Germany and a stage in European consciousness".[3] No such sense of genius reached the student in Britain. The material with which Weber dealt seemed remote from the still continuing obsession with making sense of one's field notes. The challenge to current assumptions contained in Weber's conception of *eine verstehende Soziologie* was so great that it had either to be ignored or, in the English manner, dismissed. I recall one of my tutors referring to Weber's "metaphysical interests"!

Max Weber languished on some recommended bibliographies but the student was not encouraged to make any systematic study of his works nor consequently to realise the implications of his conception of *understanding*.[4] Today there is a greater concern with the nature of social analysis and the student can still learn some of his earliest lessons in the first chapter of the *Theory of Social and Economic Organization*.[5]

The general situation in British social anthropology has not changed as much over the last ten years as one expected that it might nor to such an extent as to render the present work a "period piece". If I were allowed to alter only one section in it it would be that part which relates to "cargo cults" but, apart from the steady labour of Kenelm Burridge, the challenge of these phenomena remains unanswered.[6] More generally, as will be indicated in my discussion of the reception of Lévi-Strauss's thought, certain prejudices still linger on. Given the syllabus of the average university department of social anthropology the student will still find that the genealogy which I present provides a guide to general orientations, the more especially as the bulk of introductory works put into his hands derive from the period at which I was originally writing or from an earlier period. It is important to emphasise one feature in particular which the present work shares with these others of the same family and that is the assumption that social anthropology is essentially a post-graduate affair. If among these authors I was not the only one who had read anthropology for part of my first degree those who had were very few. What was and still is lacking is a presentation of anthropology as an education.

There are signs, however, that changes are on the way, the product of radical questionings, but these do not derive from British social anthropologists. Apart from Lévi-Strauss, whose impact I would compare to that of the creative genius in any field whose vision imposes itself as the inevitable landscape, the works of three American authors come to mind. Precisely because none of these has the international stature of Lévi-Strauss their contributions are symptomatic and it seems to me significant that they concentrate respectively on the history, the philosophy and the technique of anthropology. I have referred already to Marvin Harris's work and he together with Peter Berger and Philip Bock represent the disciplines of sociology and social anthropology as education in the sense to which I have referred and in a way which the earlier generation did not. Peter Berger's *Invitation to Sociology* is, significantly, sub-titled A Humanistic Perspective.[7] This work is, I think, essentially sound in its critical judgements and, more important, obliges the student to ask the question: "Why am I studying this subject?" We may not be entirely happy with the answers to this question which Berger suggests nor accept the sociological individual who emerges at the end of the enquiry. Nevertheless it is essential that such questions be asked and systematically examined and the book as a whole can be set beside the final chapter of *Tristes Tropiques* for comparison and discussion.[8] In a later work, in collaboration with Thomas Luckmann, Berger develops a sociology of knowledge which should be part of the apparatus of the second-year student.[9] Here again comparison with Lévi-Strauss is useful. The authors cling to the dialectic of society/culture and nature but their highly intelligent account should enable the student to take, with greater understanding, Lévi-Strauss's footnote in the final chapter of *The Savage Mind* where, after he has spoken of the reintegration of culture in nature he adds "The opposition between nature and culture to which I attached much importance at one time ... now seems to be of primarily methodological importance."[10]

If Berger usefully asks the question "Why?" another, and more recent, American production asks the question "How?" P. K. Bock's introductory work surpasses any available at the present time as a basic text.[11] Bock achieves, what one had thought impossible, the unification of the matter and method of anthropological enquiry by an emphasis upon man as meaning-maker. By this unification the author has not merely been able to discuss the technology of man which British social anthropology has for so long neglected, side by side with his categorisation of time and space and social groups but, it follows, also transcended authoritatively and finally the distinction of culture and society. From its general appearance Bock's work puts one in mind immediately of Herskovits' *Man and His Works*, which appeared in 1948, and the comparison is revealing.[12] Whereas the earlier work seemed to mark the bankruptcy of the American tradition with its persisting all-embracing tendency, the later work points to a triumphant revival.

Anybody writing about developments in British social anthropology over the last decade would be obliged to give the greater part of his attention to the impact of Lévi-Strauss. When my *Social Anthropology* was first published very little of his work was available in English. His *Structures Elementaires* and *Anthropologie Structurale* were more known about than known and what is now called "structuralism" was reflected only in the teaching of Louis Dumont and Rodney Needham at the Oxford Institute.[13] A sadly truncated English version of his *Tristes Tropiques* came out in 1961 and subsequently more works have become available.[14] His full weight has not yet been felt but the *Tristes Tropiques* together with *Totemism* and *The*

Savage Mind have probably done more than any other publications in the decade to shape the anthropologies of an increasing number of undergraduates.[15] This is true to such an extent that it is sometimes difficult to convince students, unless one refers them to the relevant correspondence and reviews, that much that they take for granted had to be fought for in the 1950s and early 60s.

I would contend that if Radcliffe-Brown established social anthropology as an academic discipline in this country it is Lévi-Strauss who has given it a vocation.

In the library of the Institute of Social Anthropology at Oxford there is an off-print of Lévi-Strauss's "Histoire et Ethnologie" which the author has inscribed by hand to Evans-Pritchard "who, by a different route, has arrived at the same destination".[16] But Lévi-Strauss's greater explicitness and formidable energy enabled him to map that route for others and to turn that destination into a base camp from which, it must be admitted, many strange expeditions have subsequently set forth.

I would insist upon *Tristes Tropiques* and *Totemism* as formative works for two connected reasons. Evans-Pritchard once wrote that the "essential difference between social anthropology and psychology is the *pons asinorum* in the learning of social anthropology".[17] For the student of our day a similar bridge is crossed a little further down the river when he has

understood why Lévi-Strauss chooses to entitle
the penultimate chapter of *Totemism* "Towards
the Intellect". The same distinction is involved
but now there is an equation of anthropology
with the intellect of man, and this intellect is
more than an intellectuality, it is man's reflexive
consciousness of himself. We could put the
matter another way by taking note of current
fashion and saying that whatever non-human
sociology may emerge from the present interest
in ethology it will not and cannot be an
anthropology; to communicate with dolphins
is not to speak with them. It is an understanding of this which enables a student to
accept the description of social anthropology
given in *Tristes Tropiques* as a vocation.[18] He
comes to recognise that it is not so much, or
not only, a profession that one *does* but also a
development of consciousness which he owes
to himself as man.

By putting my emphasis in this way I introduce a tone which may well arouse some
amusement among my British colleagues but
I am obliged to put the matter so because it is
an aspect of Lévi-Strauss which has, so to
speak, been filtered out of the British reception
of his thought. In my account of the growth of
Durkheim's influence in this country between
the two world wars I referred to Radcliffe-
Brown's somewhat narrow and selective exegesis of Durkheim's thought. I seem to see in
the writings of E. R. Leach, who was the most
effective propagandist of Lévi-Strauss's name

in the early 60s, a significantly similar selectiveness. The parallel is striking because this author seems to share with Radcliffe-Brown an epistemological confusion as to the nature of social reality. There is, running through Leach's works, a yearning for surety, for an empirical self-revelatory datum, which is at conflict with his intelligence. I attribute to this conflict the occasional tone in his writings suggestive of a more pervasive pyrrhonism. The yearning for the empirical is distinctive in the English intellectual tradition and Leach's difficulties, as they seem to me, in handling some aspects of Lévi-Strauss's thought are, therefore, representative. It is interesting on that account to consider them at a little length.

Leach has written a useful and brief account of Lévi-Strauss's work and yet, it is fair to say, he is often constrained to patronise his subject, who emerges, on occasion, as a little wild and woolly, as an idealist, a poet, a metaphysician, and as one who, to quote from an earlier article by Leach, adopts positions which are "very hard to square with materialism, empiricism or any other down to earth concern with observable facts". Leach continues, " It is this aspect of the matter which makes British social anthropologists cagey if not actively hostile."[19] Leach confesses to bias—"I am, at heart, still a functionalist"—but the consciousness of bias does not, in his case, liberate him entirely. His "reality" is on occasion susceptible to "the 'structuralist' method of Lévi-Strauss" (and let the reader ponder the significance of those inverted commas) but, where Leach fails to comprehend as, with an engaging frankness, he frequently admits to doing, then Lévi-Strauss is depicted as "a visionary ... who finds it very difficult to recognise the plain matter of fact world which the rest of us see all around". But one could develop an entire argument out of this characterisation because one way of making the case for Lévi-Strauss's peculiar importance would be to say that he has understood exactly the difficulty involved in the passage from *seeing* to *recognition.*

Can we separate, as Leach does in the passage cited and elsewhere, Lévi-Strauss the philosopher and Lévi-Strauss the anthropologist, or the methods he uses from his reason for using them? I would not think this advisable in general and in this particular case the original contribution of Lévi-Strauss to the thought of our generation is completely lost. If we preoccupy ourselves with the truth of a proposition in relation to recorded fact or the utility of a hypothesis in aiding our discovery then we are likely to be blind to the intent behind the work. I do not believe that Leach and Lévi-Strauss share the same conception of reality and therefore I think it important to take into account just what Leach categorizes as "visionary" rather than to work backwards from the coincidental agreements which occur when their differing views of reality happen to overlap. It seems more important, on the contrary, to regard Lévi-Strauss as man having his own history, not as some poetic seer whose brilliant ratiocinations occasionally produce a few useful tips. It will not do to say, as Leach says of *The Savage Mind*, that

> It often strays a long way from ordinary experience; neither Totemism nor Existentialism can be rated of central concern to the average educated Englishman.[20]

The equation of "ordinary experience" with the concerns of "the average educated Englishman" is, I take it, a pleasant joke, but it conceals an attitude of insularity hostile to intellectual growth. It is not only existentialism but also the works of the phenomenologists and the philosophical line running from Kant to Hegel which are not "rated of central concern to the average educated Englishman". But I am not confident that this is in the best interest of that gentleman's education. To dismiss as "stuff" the tradition within which and out of which Lévi-Strauss has shaped his thought is to bring our famous *empirisme anglais* one step closer to the status of euphemism.

Anyone can point to the passage in *Tristes Tropiques* where Lévi-Strauss dissociates himself from the existentialists and phenomenologists and criticises the neo-Kantians.[21] But to dissociate oneself is not to be ignorant of, it is on the contrary a kind of relation. The European philosophical tradition *is* the background *against which* Lévi-Strauss stands out to be perceived. If we cut out a two-dimensional figure and stick it upon another background it will look the clumsy piece of montage that it is.

To have some understanding of the intellectual assumptions and conflicts surrounding a young man in his late adolescence and early twenties in Paris at the mid-point between two world wars is to begin to understand something of how Lévi-Strauss represents the intellectual process. Briefly I would put the emphasis upon the capacity of the intellect to create rather than to discover. In this I follow his own argument on the opening chapter of *The Savage Mind* but at the same time I run the risk of falsification because for Lévi-Strauss discovery is creative discovery. It is important to distinguish the conception of the act of knowledge as a creative act from the assumption that it has to do with a "down to earth concern with observable facts" or the seeing of "the plain matter of fact world". I must refer the reader to Lévi-Strauss's own remark on the difference between the significant universe and the knowledge of it which I quoted in the original text (below, p. 86). In the earlier edition I said that the passage was valuable; I see now that it is critical.

If we have understood this relation of the act of knowledge to its object we cannot say, *pace* Leach, that for Lévi-Strauss "what we know is only very marginally related to what actually exists" or "that it doesn't really matter very much what kind of reality lies at the back of the verbal categories". On the contrary, the act of knowledge is becoming systematically conscious of what is really there.

But consciousness is not only consciousness *of* but, and simultaneously, consciousness *with*, it is itself a social fact. In the sentence "we understand the Nambikwara Indians", for example, the emphasis is as much upon *we* as upon *understand* and this double emphasis puts both words in a mutually qualifying relationship.

To risk a platitude: man cannot exhaust himself as the object of his own knowledge, he is perpetually making sense by destructive as well as by constructive intellectual acts. For the anthropologist it is at once the diversity and peculiarity of man that calls for sense making but this can never be in such an absolute and exhaustive way that we can totally possess this object—a man, Man, self. It does not matter at all, therefore, whether, for example, some part of Lévi-Strauss's theory which he derives from Jacobson "is now rejected by many leading linguists" so long as it makes sense of and with. It *would* matter if Lévi-Strauss argued that it made absolute sense, as though there were a "final analysis" to be made.

I think then that quite apart from his local strength and weaknesses Lévi-Strauss's peculiar achievement has been the creation of an anthropology which synthetically transcends a

number of distinct anthropologies and impresses itself upon the present generation as a new humanism. To accept that mankind exists but that humanity is still in the making is to accept an intellectual commitment which is, at the same time, free of all sentimentality or even optimism.[22]　　　　　　　　D.F.P.
University of Sussex.
January 1971.

NOTES

1. J. W. Burrow, *Evolution and Society: A study in Victorian social theory*, Cambridge University Press, 1966, p. 19 and footnote.

2. Marvin Harris, *The Rise of Anthropological Theory; A history of theories of culture*, London, 1969.

3. Trans. M. and T. Bottomore, *German Sociology*, Free Press, 1964.

4. Honourable exception must be made of the name of Dr J. G. Peristiany to whom some students in Cambridge and Oxford in the late 40s are indebted for an introduction to Weber's work.

5. Being Part 1 of *Wirtschaft und Gesellschaft*, trans. Henderson and Talcott Parsons with an introduction by the latter, London, 1947.

6. See below, p. 111, n. 71.

7. Peter L. Berger, *Invitation to Sociology; A humanistic perspective*, original American edition 1963, Pelican edition 1966.

8. Claude Lévi-Strauss, *Tristes Tropiques*, Paris, 1955.

9. Peter L. Berger and Thomas Luckmann, *The Social Construction of Reality*, London, 1967.

10. Op. cit., p. 247, footnote.

11. Philip K. Bock, *Modern Cultural Anthropology: An introduction*, New York, 1969.

12. Melville J. Herskovits, *Man and His Works*, New York, 1948.

13. Claude Lévi-Strauss, *The Elementary Structures of Kinship*, trans. Bell, von Sturmer and Needham and edited by the latter, London, 1969. *Structural Anthropology*, trans. Jacobson, New York, 1963, London, 1968.

14. *World on the Wane*, trans. Russell, London, 1961.

15. *Totemism*, trans. Needham, London, 1964. *The Savage Mind* (*La Pensée Sauvage*), trans. anon. London, 1966.

16. "Histoire et Ethnologie" in *Revue de Métaphysique et Morale*, 1949.

17. *Social Anthropology*, London, 1954, p. 46.

18. "Like mathematics or music, ethnography is one of the rare authentic vocations. One can discover it in oneself even without having been taught it." Op. cit., p. 41.

19. Edmund Leach, *Lévi-Strauss*, London, 1970. See also Leach's article in *New Left Review*, No. 34, 1966.

20. Idem, *Lévi Strauss*, p. 83.

21. *Tristes Tropiques*, pp. 44–5.

22. See Lévi-Strauss's essay "J-J. Rousseau, Fondateur des Sciences de l'Homme", in *Jean-Jacques Rousseau* (essays by various hands), A la Baconnière, Neuchatel, 1962. This is a succinct and lucid expression of Lévi-Strauss's own position and belongs, in his evolution, to the same period as *La Pensée Sauvage*.

I

Several introductions to social anthropology have appeared in the last few years, but it is still not safe to assume that the general reading public is as well acquainted with it as with the other sciences represented in this series. Part of my task, then, is to give some indication of the problems and methods of social anthropology.[1] At the same time I have to bear in mind the interests of those likely to pick up a booklet appearing under the general heading of the philosophy of science. Fortunately I am in agreement with an excellent recent statement by Peter Winch in which he criticizes the "underlabourer" conception of philosophy as follows:

> Now it is often supposed that newly developing disciplines with no settled basis of theory on which to build further research, are particularly prone to throw up philosophical puzzles; but that this is a temporary stage which should be lived through and then shaken off as soon as possible. But, in my view, it would be wrong to say this of sociology; for the philosophical problems which arise there are not tiresome foreign bodies which must be removed before sociology can advance on its own independent scientific

lines. On the contrary, the central problem of
sociology, that of giving an account of the
nature of social phenomena in general, itself
belongs to philosophy.[2]

To this extent, then, I see no division in my
task. I have, however, to remind the reader that
I am not by training a philosopher but a social
anthropologist and I cannot finally hope to
offer more than the material upon which a
philosopher might work.

Given the relatively short scope allowed to
this essay I have been obliged to choose some
device which would enable me to perform the
task proposed in the most economical manner.
I shall therefore discuss the development of
social anthropology in time and I shall see that
development as the constant interaction of
speculation about man in society, on the one
hand, and the observation of man in society, on
the other. I shall suggest that the tendency in
either the empirical or speculative approach to
claim a monopoly of truth has called for a
corrective from the other, and that the distinctive manner in which this opposition has been
transcended constitutes the individuality of
social anthropology today.

My text for this account is an observation
made by Vico which appeared—appropriately,
as will be seen—in the opening decades of the
eighteenth century:

Philosophy contemplates reason, whence
comes knowledge of the true: philology

observes the authority of human choice, whence comes consciousness of the certain.

This axiom by its second part defines as philologians all the grammarians, historians, critics, who have occupied themselves with the study of the languages and deeds of people: both their domestic affairs, such as customs and laws, and their external affairs, such as wars, peaces, alliances, travels and commerce.

This same axiom shows how the philosophers failed by half in not giving certainty to their reasonings by appeal to the authority of the philologians, and likewise how the latter failed by half in not taking care to give their authority the sanction of truth by appeal to the reasoning of the philosophers. If they had both done this they would have been more useful to their commonwealths and they would have anticipated us in conceiving this Science.[3]

A historical approach would not, however, be justified simply on the grounds of literary convenience. There is another and more important reason. The discipline as it is today *contains* its history to a remarkable degree. To put it another way, the subject is still young, is still in the process of working out a consensus of ideas, and divergences of assumption are perhaps more marked than they are in the longer established sciences. Almost inevitably, therefore, the line of development which I present is to a certain extent idiosyncratic. The dangers of this idiosyncrasy are largely overcome by a historical presentation, for any reader who goes on to acquaint himself with the writings of social anthropologists should be able to chart their position in the present from the genealogy which I present.

The term "social anthropology" itself combines two interests which correspond to the speculative and the empirical approach. Anthropology connotes the description of man and all the varieties of his behaviour; by itself it embraces an interest not only in behaviour but also in man's physical make-up and the peculiarities of races. Sociology, on the other hand, is strongly associated in many people's minds with a long tradition of speculation about the role of man in society, often closely associated with the consideration of moral problems. It is the coming together of these two, and their mutual modification, which I shall present in a historical context. In my closing pages I shall try to indicate what seems to me to be a line of development more or less implicit in the work of some leading modern social anthropologists.

Speculation about man in society is old and in that history of speculation Plato and Aristotle may appear to stand as the opposed archetypes of idealism and empiricism. Aristotle bases his *Politics* upon the observation of over a hundred and fifty constitutions known to him and his criticism of Plato (ii.v.) adduces facts in its support. But, no less than Plato, he was concerned with an ideal and the reorganization of society according to an ideal. The concern with things as they are and the concern with them as some conceive they should be, and the attempt to blend these two concerns, constitute a speculative tradition which survives into our own time. A quotation from Beatrice Webb's *My Apprenticeship* shows the vitality of this dilemma between morals and science:

> Can there be a science of social organization in the sense in which we have a science of mechanics or a science of chemistry, enabling us to forecast what will happen, and perhaps to alter the event? ... And secondly, assuming that there be, or will be, such a science of society, is man's capacity for scientific discovery the only faculty required for the reorganization of society according to an ideal? Or do we need religion as well as science, emotional faith as well as intellectual curiosity?[4]

The opposition is presented in terms characteristic of the nineteenth century, but it appears in more sober terms in the consciousness of the eighteenth century, and the steps taken at that time towards its solution mark the beginnings of the science of society.

Society could not be studied in anything resembling a scientific manner until the idea of society as in some sense an object to be studied had been established. If in the course of the sixteenth and seventeenth centuries some idea had developed that society and nature were two contradictory conditions of human existence, the achievement of the eighteenth century may finally be represented as precisely the reintegration of society in nature. That the two had been conceptually separated needs little demonstration, and the juxtaposition of two passages, the one from a manumission signed by Henry VIII in 1514 and the other being the opening passage of Rousseau's *Social Contract*, shows what had happened:

> Whereas God created all men free; but afterwards the laws and customs of nations subjected some under the yoke of servitude; we think it pious and meritorious with God to manumit, etc.
>
> Man is born free, and everywhere he is in chains. ... How did this change take place? I do not know. What can make it legitimate? To this question I hope to be able to furnish an answer.

The implication of the writ of manumission would seem to be not that the condition of servitude is in any sense an unnatural one but simply that it is a pious act to relieve it on occasion. The laws and customs of nations are here accepted as "natural" even though nature may have been qualified as a "fallen nature". More generally, social forms have, at this time, meaning in a wider and unquestioned order. But for Rousseau it is the whole order which is in question. "The social order", he continues, "is a sacred right which serves as a foundation for other rights. This right, however, since it comes not by nature, must have been built upon conventions." Society is not natural, it must therefore have some origin in man's reason, it is to that extent artificial, and reason can tell at once how it originated and how it should be organized. In short, we are still in the world of speculation where a moral assessment must be made between the natural and the social condition.*

An incisive criticism of this position had been made nearly twenty years before the publication of the *Social Contract*. David Hume, whose *Of the Original Contract* was published in 1748, noted that each of the political factions in England had raised up "a philosophical and speculative system of principles ... in order to protect and cover that scheme of actions which it pursues." The theories of original contract or of the divine origin of sovereignty were simply charters for action, they were not disinterested theories about the nature of society. We do not, for example, need to ask, he says, the reason for the obedience which men owe to their government, for society would not otherwise subsist—"This answer is clear and intelligible to all mankind."[5] Hume's disciple, Adam Ferguson, expands the argument in his *Essay on the history of Civil Society* (1767):

* I take this famous statement because it is well known and because it is representative of the period. There is more, however, to be said about Rousseau in this context. See note 9.

If we are asked therefore, Where the state of
nature is to be found? We may answer, It is
here; and it matters not whether we are
understood to speak in the island of Great
Britain, at the Cape of Good Hope, or the
straits of Magellan. ... If the palace be unnatural, the cottage is so no less; and the
highest refinements of political and moral
apprehension, are not more artificial in their
kind, than the first operations of sentiment
and reason.[6]

As far as the English school is concerned the
important contribution is the negative one:
society had been replaced in nature and become
an object of study. When we criticize the later
development of the idea that the science of
society is a *natural* science and derive this idea
from the tradition of Hume, we should not forget the value of the original thought. To anticipate a little, it is often noticed that twentieth-
century sociologists who think of themselves as
natural scientists seem to regard themselves as
immune from the pressure and influence of
society. It is only just to recall that Ferguson
anticipates this judgement when he says that
"in accounting for actions we often forget that
we ourselves have acted."[7]

After Hume and his followers modern social
anthropology finds no roots in eighteenth-
century England; the major development was in
France. Montesquieu, some twenty years
Hume's senior, published his *Spirit of Laws* in

the same year that *Of the Original Contract* appeared. It is the first consistent attempt to survey the varieties of human society, to classify and compare them and, within society, to study the interfunctioning of institutions. In the *Spirit of Laws* societies are seen as systems to be systematically analysed. But it is the attempt which is more important than the achievement. The originality of Montesquieu lies where he himself thought it lay—"My ideas are new, and therefore I have been obliged to find new words"—in his desire to heighten man's consciousness of himself in society:

> The most happy of mortals should I think myself could I contribute to make mankind recover from their prejudices. By prejudices here I mean, not that which renders men ignorant of some particular things, but whatever renders them ignorant of themselves. ...
> Man, that flexible being, conforming in society to the thoughts and impressions of others, is equally capable of knowing his own nature whenever it is laid open to his view, and of losing the very sense of it when this idea is banished from his mind.[8]

Like most people of his period, he accepted that there were certain natural laws deriving from the physical condition of man, which entails certain appetites and needs. But they are quite clearly distinguished from the positive laws, as Montesquieu calls them, which come into being once man, obeying one of the laws of his nature, associates with others in society. It is with these positive laws of religion, morality, politics and civics, which, unlike the laws of nature, are infinitely variable, that Montesquieu concerns himself. By the distinction he achieves two positions important to the advance of sociology. Firstly, although he accepts the distinction between society and nature, he is not concerned to argue that either nature or society is morally superior, since (like Hume and Ferguson in this) he does not conceive of a historical condition of man prior to society. These positive laws were to be understood in their own terms and not in terms of individual caprice or chance. This is the beginning of the idea later elaborated by Durkheim, that social phenomena constitute a *sui-generis* synthesis to which a particular science is appropriate. Secondly, Montesquieu is enabled to adopt a position of moral detachment in the face of his facts, since he is not concerned with the absolutes of nature. Introducing his work, he says that he has been misunderstood in this matter. He explains that in his use of the word *virtue* he is not speaking of Christian or of moral virtue but of political virtue, related to the establishment and maintenance of government and civil order. The morality engendered by a particular constitution is the effective morality of that constitution, but this is not to say that, therefore, morality, or Christian morality, is excluded.

Were I to say such a wheel or such a pinion is not the spring which sets the watch going, can you infer thence that it is not to be found in the watch? ... In a word, honour is found in a republic, though its spring be political virtue; and political virtue is found in a monarchical government, though it be actuated by honour.

Moral relativism is not absent in Montesquieu, but I distinguish here between the prevailing moral detachment of his work and the doctrinaire relativism of later positivists who claimed him as a precursor.

The solution of Montesquieu was not the solution of Hume and his school, but in their time both had for their effect the emergence of social man as an object, the removal of moral considerations from the study of society and some beginning of the understanding of society itself. The achievement of the eighteenth century was to be developed and distorted by a new outburst of philosophical speculation (sociology) and an increase in the uninformed but assiduous collection of facts (anthropology) in the nineteenth century. These two activities must be considered separately as they developed and before they collaborated again after the death of Auguste Comte in 1857.

In his assessment of Montesquieu, Émile Durkheim observes that after him the science of society could not progress until it had established that the laws governing society were not

different from those governing the rest of
nature and that the methods to be used for the
discovery of these laws were not different from
those of the other sciences. It was, he says,
Comte's contribution that these aims were
achieved.[9]

In fact Comte's value to us lies in his influence upon Durkheim, to which I shall refer
later. In his own time, in France and in England, his work represents a return to the tradition of moralistic speculation about society and
the attempt to deduce what man should do
from what he does. The reintegration of society
in nature seems to go hand in hand with a
yearning for some Newton of social science who
will at once support morality by unassailable
demonstration and provide an infallible guide
to future action. In the eyes of his admirers and,
later, in his own, Comte was to be the man.
Only some deep emotional need can explain the
breathless admiration of G. H. Lewes, for
instance:

> This, then, is the Positive Philosophy: the
> extension to *all* investigations of those
> methods which have been proved successful
> in the physical sciences—the transformation
> of Science into Philosophy—the condensa-
> tion of all knowledge into a homogeneous
> body of Doctrine, capable of supplying a
> Faith and consequently a Polity.[10]

Here would appear to be a theory meeting the
two criteria of Beatrice Webb, a system which

could satisfy "emotional faith as well as intellectual curiosity"—but Beatrice Webb was still
waiting well after the nineteenth century had
closed. In fact, the effect in England of Comte's
work was not to constitute any advance in the
science of society. It might even be argued that
to the extent that it was taken as a body of
doctrine, or at least an apologetic for the new
humanism, it retarded further advance. Some
people embraced the positivist religion which
Comte founded in his last years. For that intellectual circle which Beatrice Webb describes in
her autobiography, positivism did seem to
provide a hope, of which they appeared to
stand in need, that their efforts for social
reform would one day be justified by the findings of a science. But certainly Herbert Spencer,
who was not forty when Comte died, and who
may be considered as the leading English sociologist of his period, looked more to Bentham
than to Comte. He accepted Comte's new term
for the science—"sociology"—but, as we shall
see, his conception of the subject differed radic-
ally both from that of the French positivist
school and that of modern English social
anthropology, which derives in great part from
it.

In England throughout the nineteenth century a body of work which Vico would have
called philological was growing up, apparently
indifferent to any philosophical need for an all-
embracing theory. Such theory as emerges from
the work of Hume at one end and Spencer at

the other, despite the names given to it—Hume distinguished his moral philosophy from natural philosophy and Spencer called it sociology—suggests a much more vague interest in a science of man and in the possibility of a reductive analysis of human phenomena. Hume had advocated the "cautious observation of human life" but the interest of this, for him, lay in reducing "men's behaviour in company, in affairs and in their pleasures", through the operations of an introspective psychology, to their sensations. Spencer, no less, could not understand Comte's insistence that sociology, if it was to advance, must, as it were, mark out the autonomous field of its enquiries and that any positive science must refuse to reduce the phenomena of one field by explaining them in terms of another.[11] From the point of view of the present the contribution to social anthropology lay, outside France, in the growing interest, in England, Germany and America, in precisely that "cautious observation of human life", coupled with a growing knowledge of societies which lay outside any of the world's ancient civilizations—the so-called primitive peoples.

As early as 1605 Francis Bacon noted with approval the growth of what he called the history of cosmography, which was compounded of natural history and of history civil "in respect of the habitations, regiments and manners of the people ... which part of learning of all others in this latter time hath obtained most proficience." The ancients, he says, had knowledge of the Antipodes by demonstration but not in fact; they had not circled the earth as the heavenly bodies do.[12] This increase in knowledge had been substantially advanced by men like Bacon's great contemporary Richard Hakluyt, who combined a scholarly love of knowledge with a political and commercial interest in tactically useful information. His careful scrutiny and collation of travellers' reports made for an extension of the known world over the fantastic and popular world of what had been literally "traveller's tales". Also important at this time were the reports of missionaries, notably the Jesuits, who not only increased the body of knowledge available but also began to introduce, again with tactical considerations in mind, some notion of the relativity of social forms and appearances. In the eighteenth century, when they extended their activities to North and South America, they produced detailed descriptions of the tribes they encountered which today are valuable documents for the anthropologist.[12a]

Commerce, politics and missionary interests continue, in the eighteenth century, to produce increased contacts with previously unknown societies, and also what we might call the logistical considerations appropriate to each made for sober and careful observation. Finally the supposition that these societies were living in or near to a state of nature gave these observations a philosophical interest. Vico,

Montesquieu, Hume, Ferguson, Rousseau, to mention only a few, incorporated the new knowledge into their theories.

In the nineteenth century these sources of knowledge continued, and to them was added a practical concern in the government of the expanding Empire. But it is difficult to see any very specific discipline in England other than the bond provided by a growing and common interest amongst certain scholars in primitive societies, some general belief that the acquisition and classification of such knowledge was important and some sense that these researches would lead to the constitution of the natural history of mankind. When the Ethnological and Anthropological Societies were founded, in 1843 and 1863 respectively, they included in their membership physiologists concerned with the implications of racial differences, philologists in the modern sense of the word, and scholars of general antiquarian and geographical interests. As late as 1866 a Fellow of the Anthropological Society, K. R. H. Mackenzie, is content with the following account of the major divisions of anthropology:

> First, the history of mankind upon the earth ... second, a description of the existing races of men ... and third, the comparison of races structurally, geographically, and mentally *inter se*.[13]

He goes on to desiderate a fourth section "having for its special object the investigation of the interrelations between man and the cosmical bodies" in the hope of discovering, amongst other things, "that the remote stellar universe has some influence upon the qualities of food and drugs". It is not surprising that the more established disciplines looked at this new and ambitious science with doubt.

But what is interesting to note at this point in the nineteenth century in England is that although Mackenzie cites with approval Bendyshe's definition of the subject in his "History of Anthropology"[14] as an empirical science "which deals with any phenomena exhibited by collective man, and by him alone" he betrays no epistemological concern over the phrase "collective man". Comte he refers to only in defence of anthropology against the charge of encouraging atheism. The Royal Anthropological Institute as it is today, and its monthly periodical *Man*, still reflect the diverse interests which assisted at the birth of the subject. In order to understand how social anthropology developed a rather more precise view of its aims and methods we have to return to Comte, but not the extravagant and slightly crazed philosopher who inspired Harriet Martineau; rather, the precursor of Durkheim and the French sociological school.

If in England the unity of anthropology lay in the *object*—man and his works—in France there had long been a realization that this unity must be *subjectively* thought. Whatever may be advanced against the Encyclopaedists, they were as concerned with the intellectual grounds of knowledge as with the knowledge itself. No sociology emerges from the line of social philosophers which leads to Saint-Simon (1760-1825). The preoccupations were, as in England, with a natural history of man, but the contribution of the French, before Comte, was some clearer idea of how this was to be achieved. The integration of society in nature was agreed by all but to Saint-Simon is owed the analogy of human society with the physical organism; an idea which, having served its purpose, was to be a burden in the twentieth century. Society, for Saint-Simon, was not a mere collection of individuals acting according to the will of those individuals. It was a being in itself, functioning by the collaboration of its organs. Comte followed the implications of this contribution and this divides his own thought from that of the English empiricists for the same reasons as, for almost a hundred years, divided the French school of sociology from the English anthropologists. If society exists, he maintains, it must be studied positively as it exists, and the analysis of collective phenomena must preserve the integrity of their unity and not seek for explanation in terms of an introspective psychology. This is in harmony with his hierarchy of the sciences. In grading biology above physics and placing his desiderated positive sociology above biology he does not, at least before his later years, have in mind a notion of the relative excellence of these sciences; the hierarchy is a methodological one. A positive approach to experience showed that there were distinguishable areas of activity with their own effects, and it would be a violation of the facts to reduce the phenomena of one field to the laws governing another; reductive analysis of this kind Comte described as materialism.

It is important to repeat that although we may distinguish between Comte the thinker and Comte the prophet of a new religion, Comtism in the later nineteenth century inherits a confusion between the methodological division of the sciences and the doctrinaire assumption that the "higher" the science the more the *moral* superiority of its object. I shall return to this negative aspect of Comte's influence later. For the present it is sufficient to note, as between France and England in the early decades of the nineteenth century, that a mass of valuable information in England was in danger of being dissipated for the lack of intellectual discipline. The emphasis upon description was a valuable one but each observer had his own interests and convictions; he could not prevent his surmises about the effects of climate and race, psychology and the stars from imposing their categories upon his description. In this way even the value of description was threatened as philosophic and general theoretical interests increased. To be interested in man alone was not enough.

In the first decades of the nineteenth century

in England there is no figure whose work survives as of major historical importance. In America, on the other hand, first Henry Schoolcraft and later Lewis Henry Morgan, as a result of circumstances which threw them into close contact with the American Indians, had begun to make descriptive studies of their culture. To the latter in particular is owed the recognition of the importance of the study of kinship systems and his studies of them provided for many years a typology of apparently similar systems elsewhere in the world. In Germany Waitz' *Anthropologie der Naturvölker* was published in 1859, and it was selected by the Anthropological Society of London as its first publication.[15] Waitz, originally interested in psychology, characteristically suggests that his task is to write a history of mankind and that ideally this can be accomplished only by the collaboration of the zoologist, geologist, linguist, historian and psychologist. We note here again that anthropology does not emerge as a distinct discipline but only as a meeting place for several, to the extent that they share an interest in a common object—man. A sense of direction was lacking in England and this was only provided by the work of Darwin, reinforced for the student of man by the writings of Herbert Spencer. The idea that societies changed was not, of course, new, and Christian belief had provided grounds for supposing that some were better than others. However, the fragmentary nature of the material, the decay of belief and the lurking suspicion that some primitives might be both happier and better than those who studied them, made the simple application of Darwin's theories to society a welcome task. The similarities which had been noticed between such savage customs as were known and the ancient world became now explicable in terms of evolution. Differences in usage and organization in various parts of the world now became evidence which, correctly assessed, would enable the anthropologist to construct a scale which would be truly a natural history of man. The terminal point of this scale seemed evident: the mere existence of nineteenth-century European society proved its fitness to exist, and this in turn provided a sense of the moral superiority of European institutions. Darwin himself concludes his *Descent of Man* (1871) as follows:

> The astonishment which I felt on first seeing a party of Fuegians on a wild and broken shore will never be forgotten by me, for the reflection at once rushed into my mind— such were our ancestors. ... For my own part I would as soon be descended from that heroic little monkey, who braved his dreaded enemy to save the life of his keeper ... as from a savage who delights to torture his enemies, offers up bloody sacrifices, practises infanticide without remorse, treats his wives like slaves, knows no decency, and is haunted by the grossest superstitions.

Man may be excused for feeling some pride at having risen ... to the very summit of the organic scale.[16]

In this passage the moral has become fused with the physical by an intellectual process which Darwin himself could not, perhaps, have explained. The man to whom he permits modest pride is no longer the human species, but Darwin himself and his evolved contemporaries.

It was less easy to determine the point of origin and the subsequent development. Private property, monogamous marriage, inheritance through the paternal line, the State and monotheism were variously derived according to the bias of the writer. Given the European institution, the usual procedure was to posit, if no evidence was forthcoming, its opposite, thus: for monotheism—no religion; for marriage—sexual promiscuity. Next after these could reasonably be placed that form of primitive practice which least resembled the European—a belief in evil spirits, or matriarchal society. In this way evidence from different parts of the world and from ancient literature were brought together; steps for which no evidence could be found were surmised. The belief that it was the business of the anthropologist to trace the evolution of human customs survived well into the twentieth century. As late as 1927 Peake and Fleure, inaugurating their series *The Corridors of Time*, could write:

The extension of Charles Darwin's point of view to the interpretation of civilization is one of the most far reaching changes in the intellectual life of our time.[17]

Such reaction as there was to this assumption is characterized under the name of diffusionism. The work of F. Ratzel (1844-1904) and F. Gräbner (1877-1934) in Germany vigorously opposed simple ideas of unilinear evolution. They showed how the statistical study of culture traits suggested the adoption of customs and the borrowing of technical inventions which effectively prevented the discovery of any single line of development. In fact by the 1890's the crude application of Darwin's theories had been considerably modified and the fact of diffusion was taken into account, as indeed it always had been by men who had some sensitivity to the facts that they studied. It is their concern for the "authority of human choice" which establishes the value of the English anthropologists of this period, rather than their speculative concerns. If the concern with origins led them to consider the facts of primitive society as they knew them from literature, their analysis of those facts and the vocabulary which they elaborated is not often vitiated by theoretical concerns. Sir Henry Maine's book *Ancient Law*, published in 1861, brought a legal mind to bear upon Indo-European institutions and his distinction—between societies based up-on status, where social activity was determined by hereditary membership of and position in a group of kinsmen, and societies based upon contract between relatively free individuals—remains a useful concept. Today we are no longer concerned to argue that status necessarily precedes contract and recognize that the two notions are not incompatible in one and the same society. In Maine's work we can excise the genetical argument and still profit from the discussion that remains. This can be said of many writers of the period, but even this patronizing judgement is superseded by the recognition that Maine and his most able contemporaries allowed themselves to be guided, by such facts as were available, to combat the products of more speculative evolutionism. He saw, for example, nothing in his facts which could lead him to agree with the popular fantasy that all societies had evolved from a condition of sexual promiscuity through a matriarchal period to a condition of society laying its main emphasis upon descent through males. Of Tylor (1832-1917) and Frazer (1854-1941), the best-known figures outside the subject, much the same may be said. Their works are read today not from any concern with the stages of development which they tried to establish but as introductions to the variety of human phenomena and for the argument over terminology, which rested upon a slowly increasing knowledge, if still at secondhand, of the facts. A simple example demonstrates the value of this kind of discussion. The earlier and rationalistic supposition had been that all beliefs and actions which appeared to rest upon the existence of beings outside the world of "nature" were to be classed together as super-stitions. The objection to any such belief was such that few were concerned to discriminate the degrees of objection. Frazer, no less con-vinced that science would free man from any such dependence upon supernatural forces, was led by his preoccupation with evolution to dis-tinguish magic from religion and to adduce different kinds of behaviour corresponding to the two categories. For magic, being morally, as he saw it, inferior, must have preceded religion and given place to it just as (and the argument is, of course, characteristic of the period) religion would give way to science. Tylor, on the other hand, was on surer ground, as far as later evidence shows, in distinguishing the two in order to derive the origins of each. Religion, for him, was not a sophisticated form of magic but had its origins in the human psyche, in primitive man's dreams, which pro-duced a belief in some sort of soul and the extension of this belief to inanimate nature. From this theory we have the word "animism", which is still used by non-anthropologists to characterize primitive religions. Magic, on the other hand, he characterized as primitive science resting on a faulty knowledge of the nature of things.

Although, then, extremists appear to have wasted much intellectual energy in proving evolutionary scales, the real value of the period in England seems to lie in a growing pre-occupation with fact, and the subsequent development of terminology and conceptual distinctions. These in their turn showed how inconclusive the argument must remain while scholars had to rely upon the fragmentary reports of others.

Two interrelated criticisms remain to be made. Although we may disregard the evolutionist framework in the works of these early anthropologists and derive profit from their discussions, we cannot say that as yet there existed a concern with society as such. Secondly, the emphasis is always finally upon the individual institution, the individual custom. Frazer, it will be remembered, built up his vast survey of beliefs and customs all over the world and in the past, *The Golden Bough*, upon his interest in one isolated custom—the slaying of the priest-king by his successor. For others it was the institution of the family, or marriage, which constituted the problem. The idea was not yet accepted that these customs or institutions were connected with others and formed a complex of meaning for the particular peoples who maintained them. If people in different parts of the world like to jump over bonfires at the end of their harvest the action alone does not necessarily imply the same intention, the same meaning. That the preoccupation with individuals led away from meaning appears as well in the work of those who called themselves diffusionists. For them it was enough to counter a theory of the independent evolution of some institution by showing that it had spread, or might have spread, from one centre by human contact. The diffusionist corrective was important but here again the mapping of isolated individual examples of custom or material culture was more important for them than the consideration of the social contexts in which objects and beliefs had value and meaning for people. The failure, then, to consider society, as opposed to parts of society, was leading thought away from fact to a new speculative interest.

This lack of a sociological approach, the concern with the individual, had the effect that we have noted earlier in the century. What we should now recognize as social phenomena were reduced by explanation in terms of other sciences. And it was almost inevitable that the sciences which seemed to provide the best terms for the discussion of human behaviour were the sciences of the individual, then more closely related—biology and psychology. We may take Herbert Spencer as the most systematic thinker in this field at the time. Reluctant to appear intellectually indebted to anyone, he nevertheless saw the value of Comte's new term "sociology" and adopted it. His projected *Synthetic Philosophy* included three volumes on *The Principles of Sociology*, and first began to appear in book form in 1879. In a slighter work published a few years earlier, *The Study of Sociology*

(1873), we get a comprehensive view of the place of Spencerian sociology in the whole scheme that he proposed. The book represents Spencer at his best, more concerned to argue the need and value of social science before a general intelligent public than to dogmatize and attack his fellow specialists. He discusses the need for a science of society and shows amusingly and subtly the difficulties of such a science—the biases of education, patriotism, class, and political and theological affiliations which hamper the sociologist in arriving at an objective view as Spencer understood it. But just as in the elaboration of his *Synthetic Philosophy* biology and psychology had preceded sociology, so, in this introduction to his subject, he argues the need for a preparation in biology and psychology for the understanding of social phenomena. Comte had not recognized the introspective psychology of his time as a science but he did give a logical priority to biology in his hierarchy of sciences; there, however, the similarity ends. Spencer holds to his axiom that "the natures of the units necessitate certain traits in the aggregates":

> Given the structures and the consequent instincts of the individuals as we find them, and the community they form will inevitably present certain traits; and no community having such traits can be formed out of individuals having other structures and instincts.[18]

Later, speaking of the necessary preparation in biology, he associates Adam Ferguson with Comte and singles out of the latter's conception of social phenomena "his recognition of the dependence of Sociology on Biology".[19] It is difficult not to conclude that this is a perverse humour on Spencer's part. Comte, acquainted with the work of Hume and his followers, had seen clearly that the composition of an aggregate does not determine the manner in which that aggregate, as a fact in itself, should be studied. His sociology was to study social life as the biologist studied natural life but it was not to seek for biological or psychological explanations of its data.[20] The diversity of social institutions could not be explained from the unity of human instincts, and, conversely, if we were to find human beings "having other structures and instincts", we could only account for the difference in terms of the difference in community. Spencer's view is an instance of what Comte meant by "materialism". From it the only development could be a search for the lowest common denominator beneath the variety of appearances, a common denominator already given in the term "human instincts". The argument against Spencer is not dead; the same epistemological objection is still levelled by modern social anthropology against either the attempt to explain social phenomena in terms of individual psychology, or the basically materialist analysis which, refining only slightly on Spencer, discards what is distinctive in any society in order to reduce it to pre-established, and usually economic, categories. Such an approach leads to a comparative sociology of which the end is a set of lowest common denominators as uninteresting as they are predictable from the outset of the enquiry.

Owing to a lack of discipline and to Spencer's influence anthropologists in England in the nineteenth century concerned themselves with individual items of cultures and, when they moved away from description, were content with explanations of a psychological nature. The French sociological school, to which I now turn, was not to have any major effect on this way of thinking until after the war of 1914-18.

Émile Durkheim was born in 1858 and founded, in 1896, the *Année sociologique*, which, until 1913, provided reviews of current publications and many original articles by Durkheim and the small group of scholars whom he had attracted. In addition to the volumes of the *Année* his most important works include *The Division of Labour* (1893), *The Rules of Sociological Method* (1895), *Suicide* (1897), *The Elementary Forms of Religious Life* (1912), all of which have been translated into English. He inspired and instructed a brilliant group of colleagues which was crushed by the Great War. When the *Année* was resumed in 1923 the survivors, Hubert, Mauss and Bouglé, record the deaths of Durkheim himself and of almost all his most promising pupils, including his son.

Nevertheless, sociology in France continued the Durkheimian impetus until the Second World War and the death of Marcel Mauss in 1950.

Much of what Durkheim said has been misinterpreted, even by some foreign admirers, and yet his exposition is always clear.[21] His business was to revive the conception of sociology put forward by Comte, without taking over the speculative method. Durkheim never relinquished the idea that sociology had a moral role to play in the consciousness of society but he never seems to have believed that it would achieve mandatory laws.

Before considering the advance towards a social anthropology which occurs with the work of Durkheim and his colleagues it might be as well to deal with two of his terms which are frequently misrepresented in simplicist accounts of his theory: the idea of collective consciousness and the often-repeated slogan that social facts must be studied as things, *comme des choses*. The first is often taken to mean a belief in an existing group mind or *Volksgeist*; the second is usually offered as an example of Durkheim's "materialism". Since the first charge would come under the head of "idealism" it is often difficult to understand how one critic can sometimes accuse the one man of both.

Durkheim's formal statement concerning collective representations is found in an article published in 1898 in which he is dealing

primarily with the psychological arguments of
William James.[22] He was already acquainted
with the work of German scholars and the tendency to postulate some kind of group mind.
P. Bastian (1826-1905), for example, had spent
some ten years of his youth in travel in Australia, America, the Far East and the Pacific.
His study of man and his customs was much in
the tradition of Hume in that he also sought the
final explanation in terms of the nervous system.
There were, he considered, certain basic
notions (*Elementargedanken*) common to all men;
these were varied only by the geographical
circumstances in which man found himself, and
these variations Bastian called group ideas
(*Völkergedanken*). In this tradition also was a
younger man of whose teaching Durkheim had
first-hand experience, W. Wundt, who was to
publish his *Völkerpsychologie* in 1900. It is
precisely against such positions, fully conscious
of their implications, that Durkheim was
arguing.

But there is, in the history of thought, an
older, and in a sense wider, tradition, in which
Durkheim seems to have a place. In his preoccupations (and even in the works of Comte)
we find echoes of the seventeenth-century con-
troversy, one-sided as it was, between Leibnitz
and Locke which arose from the latter's *Essay
on the Human Understanding*. Locke's system, says
Leibnitz, "bears more relation to Aristotle,
mine to Plato", and he characterizes the debate
as follows:

Our differences are on subjects of some importance. The question at issue is whether the soul itself is entirely void, like a tablet whereon nothing has yet been written (*tabula rasa*), as is the view of Aristotle and the author of the Essay, and everything marked on it comes solely from the senses and from experience, or whether the soul contains originally the principles of various notions, which external objects simply recall from time to time, as is my view and that of Plato.[23]

It is not, of course, in these terms that Durkheim is concerned to argue. As far as the origin of understanding is concerned, he would almost certainly have agreed with Locke. But passing from the consideration of origin to that of "nature", Durkheim stands with Leibnitz and with Leibnitz' use of the word "representation". Allowing for the theological terms in which the argument is cast, we can see clearly in the following passage an anticipation of the positivist refusal of reductive analysis, and characterization of it as materialism.

Experience is necessary I allow for the soul to be determined to such and such particular thoughts, and for it to take notice of the ideas which are in us. But by what means can the senses and experience provide ideas? Has the soul windows? Does it resemble a tablet? Is it like wax? It is evident that all those who speak thus of the soul treat it at bottom as corporeal. I shall have brought against me the axiom, accepted among the philosophers, that *there is nothing in the soul save that which comes from the senses.* But we must except the soul itself and its affections. *Nihil est in intellectu, quod non fuerit in sensu;* excipe, *nisi ipse intellectus.* (There is nothing in the intellect which was not previously in the senses; provided we make the reservation, except the intellect itself.)[24]

The almost irreconcilable differences of Locke and Leibnitz continued and continue to divide students of society and produce strange alliances. It is of more than historical interest to note the famous debate between Macaulay and James Mill when we recall Mill's criticism of Comte. Arguing that Comte had made a science of society possible but had not created it (a proposition with which one might agree for different reasons), Mill says:

In social phenomena the elementary facts are feelings and actions, and the laws of these are the laws of human nature, social facts being the results of human acts and human situations. Since, then, the phenomena of man in society result from his nature as an individual being, it might be thought that the proper mode of constructing a positive Social Science must be by deducing it from the general laws of human nature, using the facts of history merely for verification. Such, accordingly, has been the conception of social science by many of those who have endeavoured to render it positive, particularly by the school of Bentham. M. Comte considers this an error.[25]

In 1829, in debate with Mill and, later, Bentham, Macaulay seems to anticipate Mill's observations and the following passage reads like an immediate answer to them:

We blamed Mr Mill for deducing his theory of government from the principles of human nature. "In the name of Sir Richard Birnie and all saints" cried Mr Bentham, "from what else should it be deduced?" ... we shall venture to answer Mr Bentham's question by another. How does he arrive at those principles of human nature from which he proposes to deduce the science of government? ... He will say—By experience. But what is the extent of this experience? Is it an experience which includes the conduct of men entrusted with the powers of government? If it includes experience of the manner in which men act when entrusted with the powers of government, then those principles of human nature from which the science of government is to be deduced can only be known after going through that inductive process by which we propose to arrive at the science of government. Our knowledge of human nature, instead of being prior in order to our knowledge of the science of government, will be posterior to it.[26]

It is in this tradition that Durkheim was to argue for the validity of human experience, "the authority of human choice", over against speculative derivations from human nature, and for a mode of analysis which preserves that experience and does not reduce it. If we substitute society and individual for intellect and senses in Leibnitz' dictum we have Durkheim's position: There is nothing in society which was not previously in the individuals, except the society itself.

In the discussion of individual and collective representations to which I have referred Durkheim is defending the *sui-generis* quality of both mind and society against sensational psychology. The mind is not an epiphenomenon of the nervous system and the demonstration of its neural basis does not destroy the relative autonomy of mental phenomena once they exist. We have to remember that it was possible at that time for James to say that "memory is not a fact of the mental order at all". Arguing by analogy (and he is careful to insist that he is doing so), Durkheim maintains that just as the human mind, once it has come into being, obeys its own laws, so the interaction of individual people in society produces certain effects which, once formed, cannot be discovered in any one particular individual mind. One distinctive association of ideas, as opposed to a general theory of association, cannot be explained in terms of a neural base: one particular system of religious beliefs, shall we say, as opposed to a general theory of religion, cannot be explained in terms of the psychology of the individuals believing them. Durkheim maintains that if there is to be a collective psychology it is, quite simply, sociology, and much confusion would be saved by thus distinguishing it from psychology, which has always been considered as the science of the individual mind. He concludes:

> Beyond the ideology of the psycho-sociologist and the materialistic naturalism of the socio-anthropologist* there is room for a sociological naturalism which would see social phenomena as specific facts, and which would undertake to explain them while preserving a religious respect for their specificity.[27]

His "collective consciousness" is, then, not a postulate or hypothesis but simply a descriptive term arrived at polemically and by analogy. It refers to the fact that the ideas prevailing in a group at a given moment can only be understood in relation to each other and lose their specificity when they are broken down into the variety of motives and meanings which each individual attaches to them. We can illustrate Durkheim's position more clearly by referring to his rejection of the statistical analysis of morality. The average man, the majority of a total population, may for a time not feel at all, or feel only slightly, the moral rules which play their part in making that society what it is. But it does, therefore, not follow that these moral

* He has Spencer chiefly in mind.

rules do not exist—and indeed, the action of one individual is sufficient sometimes to show their vitality in that society.

The objection to the injunction that social facts must be studied as things is more simply disposed of. Durkheim may speak for himself. In the preface to the second edition of his *Rules of Sociological Method* he notes that the phrase had been regarded as paradoxical and scandalous, an attempt to assimilate social life to the realities of the exterior world. He replies that on the contrary he is trying to vindicate the reality of social life:

> What in fact is a thing? A thing is opposed to an idea as that which one knows from without is opposed to that which one knows from within. A thing is any object of knowledge ... of which we cannot achieve an adequate notion by a simple act of mental analysis, anything which the mind cannot understand except by going outwards, by observation, experimentation, and by passing progressively from the external and immediately accessible characteristics to the less visible and more profound ones. To treat facts of a certain order as things is not therefore to classify them in this or that category of reality; *it is to adopt towards them a certain mental attitude.*[28]

These two notions are closely connected, not so much as a theory, but as a method. No one individual in a society, says Durkheim, contains within himself all the currents of thought, often contradicting each other, which animate that society. The individual is not aware of the interrelations of the institutions which control his life. He cannot, therefore, by a simple act of introspection arrive at the truth about society. Durkheim's definition of the term "social phenomena", the idea that collective representations are to be understood as if they were outside the individual and hence studied as if they were things, echoes the earlier pronouncement of Renouvier: "The two words 'representation' and 'thing', at first distinguished, meet and blend in a third term—'phenomenon'."[29]

The idea of the specificity of different levels of phenomena and the kind of science appropriate to them is central to Durkheim's thought. Each *sui-generis* synthesis was also a creative synthesis which in turn produced specific phenomena. The relation of a particular religion to the institutions of a particular society had to be studied, but this was only a part of the task. The system of belief and action which constituted the religion had also its own relative autonomy and (although Durkheim envisaged this as the work of the future) one may still discern in his thought the possibility of a phenomenology of religions.

These points need to be stressed when one is concerned with the contribution of Durkheim, for he himself often seems carried away by language to speak of society as acting and thinking.

Nor did he ever entirely emancipate himself from the dream of sociology as a future basis for rational legislation. But even so there is little of the brash optimism that one associates with the school of Saint-Simon, the emphasis being rather upon the value of increased knowledge.

He has also suffered at the hands of some admirers. The Comtian analogy of society with the natural organism was dismissed in the *Année sociologique* as a notion which had served its purpose and become an obstacle to thought;* it was nevertheless maintained well into the present century by some English social anthropologists. The idea that Durkheimian analysis involves the reduction of religious phenomena to some kind of social substratum in the Marxian manner is still quite prevalent.

As opposed to the all-embracing concerns of the English anthropologists, Durkheim was concerned at the outset to define what he meant by social facts and his argument to this end is a good example of his manner. If, he says, we look at the current use of the term "social

---

* This occurs in a review of Lorenz von Stein's *Eine Kritik der organischen methode in der Sociologie* (Berlin, 1898). The value of the organic method is recognized in the discoveries it has provoked, but the reviewers admit that to pass from the comparison of societies with organisms to the identification of the two is to fail to recognize the specificity of social laws. Social facts, singularly more complex than natural facts, obey a teleological necessity rather than a mechanical one. Sociology holds a middle place between the "sciences of laws" and the "sciences of events". It discovers rules and rhythms rather than laws. (*Année sociologique*, vol. 2 (1897-8), pp. 159-60.)

fact", we find that it implies an interest in almost all the phenomena that take place in society—and there is no human activity which is not social. Each individual drinks, eats and sleeps and exercises his reason. Society can be seen to maintain and regularize these activities. If these facts are to be considered social facts then sociology has no proper field of study which is not already that of biology and psychology. But in fact man has certain roles to play and certain duties to perform which are defined by law and custom and which do not depend upon the existence of this or that particular man or even his willingness to recognize them. A whole body of religious, legal, commercial and linguistic systems exist outside the individual whether he is conscious of them or not, whether he uses them or not. These systems are not only in this sense outside the individual; they have also a coercive power upon him. He may act according to certain rules quite gladly, but this does not make these rules less objective or less coercive, as he discovers if he tries to deviate from them. The punishment of crime is an obvious example, but the reaction of society —the derision of others, and even their casual avoidance of one—has the same effects as a penalty in the ordinary sense. These facts, then, are not to be confused with organic phenomena (since they consist in representations and in acts), nor with psychic phenomena, which exist only in the consciousness of the individual. They can properly be called social facts, because their substratum is not the individual but the various aggregates within society—the religious, political, professional, literary societies which make up the total society. However, these rules which are relatively precise and depend upon some degree of organization are not the only social facts. There are the less crystallized but no less objective and coercive social currents—movements of enthusiasm, indignation, etc.—which do not originate in one particular individual conscience. Again, the fact that we may be caught up in such a movement may make us unaware of social pressure. A crude example is provided by the atrocities sometimes performed by a crowd composed of otherwise harmless individuals. When the crowd disperses the individual has a sense of moving from one world into another. And what is true of passing explosions of public excitement is equally true of more durable movements which constantly occur throughout the society or in some part of it—such are the shifts in religious and political opinion, in art and in fashion. The study of education shows how society, acting through the parents, constrains the child to sleep, eat and generally act in the manner which that society approves. The constraint is less apparent as the child grows up, since constraint gives birth to habits. The constraint is more refined but does not cease to exist. Although Durkheim points to generality as a defining feature of social facts, he concludes by qualifying this criterion. Thoughts and actions common to all the members of a society or to a majority are not social because general but general because social. This is shown by the fact that systems of belief and rules of different kinds are refracted only partially in each individual, and some are no less efficacious because they are practised by a minority.

Some obvious problems arise from Durkheim's position, notably in his conception of the individual as a social being and in the connected presentation of society as static. At the time he was writing, however, it was precisely the transcendance of society over the individual which had to be stressed. This stress had two important effects. First, it eliminated arguments either as to the nature or to the origin of social institutions which were supposed to rest upon man's presumed "natural" fear, aggression, and sexual or material acquisitiveness. In the tradition of Montesquieu, it neither affirmed nor denied the existence of these inherent qualities; it argued their irrelevance. Secondly, but more slowly, it undermined the interest in social evolution. Durkheim himself, in the second volume of the *Année*, considered the search for origins a necessary task for the sociologist: "To know how something is constituted we have to discover how it has been constituted." But in fact nothing is so confused in his various writings as his conception of this task. At times he uses the word "primitive" to mean "earliest chronologically", at others to mean the most simple form of some phenomenon according to criteria which it is not easy to understand. Occasionally he appears to argue that to have discovered the origin of something is at the same time to know its "nature", and then he proceeds to deny that this is so. For example, in justifying his interest in the sociology of religion he says that this is because so many important institutions of modern society were in their first form religious. "A multitude of problems change their aspect completely from the moment that one sees their connection with the sociology of religion." Nature and origin seem close here, but Durkheim then adds a footnote which suggests quite the contrary and would seem even to undermine the whole of his argument about the relative autonomy of different levels of synthesis. The relevance of the sociology of religion, he says,

... does not at all imply that religion should play the same role in modern society that it played before. In a sense the contrary conclusion would be better founded. Precisely because religion is a primitive fact, it should more and more give place to the new social forms which it has engendered. To understand these new forms we have to connect them with their religious origins without confusing them with religious facts properly so called. In the same way in the individual, sensation is the primitive fact from which the superior intellectual functions have developed ... it does not follow that the mind of a cultivated adult, particularly today, is made up only of sensations. On the contrary their role diminishes as intelligence develops.[30]

The passage is characteristic and his analogy is disastrous, coming from a man concerned to show the irrelevance of biological explanations in the study of social phenomena.

Confused as he himself may have been, the emphasis upon society and the interconnectedness of social institutions, beliefs and practices made it increasingly difficult to isolate one custom or belief from its social context in order to trace its evolution, while, on the other hand, the evolution of one total society was not easily to be studied. Durkheim did not concern himself much with the demonstration of origins and such stages as do emerge, in, for instance, *The Division of Labour*, are rather more analyses of the compatibility and incompatibility of certain beliefs and institutions, e.g., the incompatibility of segmentary and industrial societies.

Until the 1914-18 War Durkheim and his colleagues continued to publish their own work and to evaluate and discuss the work of others in the successive volumes of the *Année sociologique*. The historical test of what was achieved under Durkheim's leadership is that the body of their works continues to be read and argued over as a living classic while it is difficult to think of a single contemporary in England who receives a degree of the same attention. The French sociologists shared with the English anthropologists their lack of first-hand observation; both relied upon the reports of others, which were not always reliable. Durkheim's students who were to inaugurate field observations were, as we have seen, killed in the First World War. Nevertheless, the establishment of a sociology in France enabled Durkheim and his school to work more effectively upon this second-hand material. Marcel Mauss, who developed Durkheim's thought and showed himself to have more power of perception and imagination, influenced a whole later generation of social anthropologists. Célestin Bouglé, employing the material provided by English Government officials in India, produced in the early 1900's a work on caste which, as a general treatment of the subject, has not yet been surpassed even by writers with many years of experience in India.

Viewed against a nineteenth-century background, Durkheim and the *Année sociologique* performed an invaluable service, but it is impossible not to recognize that as the word "society" looms larger, notably in Durkheim's own writings, there is danger of a new speculative sociologism which could only be corrected by a return to observation. The value of first-hand experience had been demonstrated by Morgan much earlier and both in Germany and England the work of men like Bastian, Ratzel, Tylor and Frazer was producing a growing appreciation of the need for field-work. The first attempt to study a people in the light of current theory was that of Franz Boas, a German, who later took American citizenship and founded American anthropology on a sound basis. He had studied under Wundt, but his original approach was typical of the German human geographers of the time: the effect of habitat upon man was all-important and played a determining role in forming his institutions. Boas set out in the early 1880's to study the Eskimo of Cumberland Sound in accordance with this theory. Perhaps more by necessity than by inclination, he adapted himself to the Eskimo manner of living and was led to experience that dependence upon the people which is one of the most valuable parts of field-work. He devoted the greater part of his life, after he had settled in America, to his Eskimo studies, embracing their customs, language, artifacts and physiology. In England the period of systematic field-work was inaugurated by A. C. Haddon, who led a team, composed of various specialists, to the Torres Straits with the intention of making as exhaustive a study as possible of every aspect of native life there. The fact that the expedition was made, its ambition and its results, seem to sum up the history of English anthropology at the end of the nineteenth century. Haddon, originally a zoologist, and Rivers, neurologist and psychologist, were both of about the same age as Durkheim. The irony of the situation is that Durkheim appears to have had a better understanding of the anthropological facts upon

which he increasingly relied and yet showed no
interest in finding out what they were really
like. The English expedition produced a mass of
facts and valuable museum collections, but
lacked an intellectual discipline to inform the
diverse interests of its members. But the new
knowledge of primitive beliefs and customs, of
artifacts and music, established the value of
such experience for individual researchers.
Two anthropologists were made out of the
expedition—W. H. Rivers and C. G. Seligman,
who had joined to study primitive pathology
and medicine. To Rivers is owed the encourage-
ment of field-work and the stress on its capital
importance for the anthropologist. His theoretical position represents little advance in the
subject. He conceived the business of anthropology, as did Haddon, to be the reconstruction
of a natural history and later he adhered to the
cause of the extremists of the diffusionist school.
Towards the end of his life he could write that
the end of any enquiry into social behaviour
was its explanation in terms of psychology.
C. G. Seligman, equally interested in the all-
embracing study of man, continued to carry
out and to encourage field-work from London.
The blend of all the diverse interests and
assumptions which had crept in under the now
vast anthropological umbrella is reflected in his
work, but his apparent refusal to commit himself to premature theoretical positions gave him
influence over a generation which was to reject
Rivers. In London he taught Malinowski,

whose field-work during the First World War marks the break with general anthropology. More important is his field-work, conducted with his wife, B. S. Seligman, in the Sudan over the years 1909-12 and 1921-2, which resulted in the publication of *Pagan Tribes of the Nilotic Sudan* in 1932. This descriptive demarcation of a whole cultural and linguistic area provided a factual background which was to be filled in by the more intensive field-work of E. E. Evans-Pritchard, now Professor of Social Anthropology at Oxford, during the 'thirties, to be followed by other researchers in the years after the Second World War. The result has been not only a descriptive coverage as yet unequalled in any other area, but also a major stimulus to research workers elsewhere.

II

The two personalities who were to dominate social anthropology between the two world wars, and in great part to create it as we know it today, were Malinowski and Radcliffe-Brown. The first, student of Frazer and Westermarck, and of Seligman in London, was in Australia when war broke out in 1914. As an "enemy alien" he was subject to confinement, but had the good fortune to be detained in his chosen field, the Trobriand Islands. He was in this way enabled to have as full an experience of primitive life as any field-worker could wish. Instead of the cursory survey which was until then the conventional notion of field-work, he was able, over four years, to learn the language of the Trobrianders and to enter into more intimate relationships with them than had hitherto been possible for any anthropologist. Today a period of two years, even with a break of a few months in the middle, is considered a suitable period for one piece of field-work. But the degree of intimacy, the involvement in local life, the emotional and even material dependence upon the people which Malinowski achieved through his blend of good and bad fortune, have remained as ideals of good field-work. His students, who conducted research in the Pacific and Africa in the late 'twenties and through the 'thirties, prided themselves precisely upon the extent to which they were "accepted" by the people they studied, and to the extent that they were able to dissociate themselves from European governmental and missionary activities and even from the material symbols and comforts which might act as a barrier between them and as full as possible an engagement in native life.

Malinowski's works were followed by the publication of material by his students far superior in detail and in subtlety to anything that had appeared before. And inevitably participation in an alien social life produced an awareness of complexity and depth which in turn made for a radical revaluation of terminologies based upon second-hand reports, or, at best, the superficial observations of a few months. Characteristic of the advice which Malinowski gave is the following from one of his earliest works. Saying that it is pleasant to have some European centre where one can go in time of sickness and for stores he goes on:

> But it must be far enough away not to become a permanent milieu in which you live and from which you emerge at fixed hours only to "do the village". It should not even be near enough to fly to at any moment for recreation. For the native is not the natural companion for the white man, and after you have been working with him for several hours, seeing how he does his gardens, or letting him tell you items of folk-lore, or discussing his customs, you will naturally hanker after the company of your own kind. But if you are alone in a village beyond reach of this, you go for a solitary walk for an hour or so, return again and then quite naturally seek out the natives' society, this time as a relief from loneliness, just as you would any other companionship. And by means of this natural intercourse, you learn to know him. ... [31]

Field-work became in this way not merely the study of things from the outside, but an emotional and moral engagement in the life of the people studied. The experience of the people themselves comes to have priority over the theoretical preoccupations of the observer.

But Malinowski's gifts as a field-worker were not matched by any gift for systematic thought. His name is associated primarily with the term "functionalism" as a result of his plea in 1926 for a theory of a "purely empirical nature" for modern field-work. The functional analysis was to aim

> ... at the explanation of anthropological facts at all levels of development by their function, by the part which they play within the integral system of culture, by the manner in which they are related to each other within the system, and by the manner in which this system is related to the physical surroundings. It aims at the understanding of the nature of culture, rather than at conjectural reconstructions of its evolution or of past historical events ...[32]

Reiterating this in 1931, he pointed out how necessary it was to study a culture or society "in its own right ... as a self-contained reality". This seems almost a truism to-day, but at the time the assumptions of evolutionists and diffusionists were still dominant. Such theories had a bad influence upon field-work, for their proponents viewed the elements of culture as extraneous to their contexts, either relating them in time to an evolutionary scale, or relating them in space upon some diffusionist map. But beyond this vigorous insistence upon the interrelatedness of social facts it is difficult to derive any formal functionalist theory of society from Malinowski's works. He employs the word "function" itself in a variety of ways: sometimes to refer to the fact of interrelatedness, sometimes to the pervasive influence of one activity (economics, for instance) upon many institutions, sometimes with reference to a theory of biological and emotional needs, so that the function of an institution becomes the part it plays in satisfying these needs. But today nobody reads Malinowski for his theories; his field monographs, on the other hand, despite their turgid and romantic style, remain as masterpieces of field-work and provide an account of one people which for its detail has not been equalled.

In his first major publication after the experience of prolonged field-work, Malinowski does not develop any theory which precisely defines the difference between him and the writers who had preceded him. But his attitude was to harden rapidly in a few years, probably under the influence of Radcliffe-Brown, who saw much earlier the incompatibility of sociology and natural history. Throughout his life, however, Malinowski never realized the full implications of the sociological position and drew indifferently upon sociological, psychological and finally biological theories. Once he had so effectively and sensitively stressed the importance and nature of the field-work experience there still remained a need for a more consistent, a more precise discipline which would be able to order the new mass of facts which were being collected. Radcliffe-Brown represents speculation over against Malinowskian empiricism in the period between the two world wars.

The influence of Radcliffe-Brown's theories upon the assumptions of a whole generation was immense and it is therefore necessary, even in a limited space, to attempt to sort out the dominant themes of his thought, before one can evaluate his contribution.

His first major and probably most lasting work is his report of the field-work conducted in the Andamans called *The Andaman Islanders*.[33] The history of the publication gives an entry to the intellectual ambience in which the author found himself. It was published in 1922, but in a Preface to the 1933 edition Radcliffe-Brown writes:

> In 1908-9, when the writing of this book was undertaken, anthropologists and ethnologists were concerned either with formulating hypotheses as to the origins of institutions or with attempts to provide hypothetical reconstructions of the details of culture history. ... It was largely from this point of view that I approached the study of the Andaman Islanders. ... During the course of my work a systematic examination of the methods available for such reconstructions of the unknown past convinced me that it is only in extremely rare cases that we can ever

approach demonstrable conclusions and that speculative history cannot give us results of any real importance for the understanding of human life and culture.[34]

He goes on to contrast the interests of these "historical ethnologists" with the work of the French sociologists and the use to which they had put ethnological data. From them he derives a sense of the importance of the meaning which social behaviour has for the members of the observed society, as opposed to the meaning which the observer might attach to it. Connected with this is the function of particular beliefs and institutions. For instance:

> We cannot discuss the social function of mythology or ritual without an understanding of the meanings of particular myths and ritual actions.[35]

But even while distinguishing meaning and function, Radcliffe-Brown begins to reduce the former to the latter. The search for "meaning" becomes an obvious expedient of research. One must learn a culture as one learns a language and not impose upon the mere appearances the significance which they might have in one's own society. "Function", on the other hand, becomes the sociological meaning which (and increasingly in his work) swallows up the subjective meaning of social phenomena. Having discussed the importance of meaning, Radcliffe-Brown goes on immediately to write:

The notion of function in ethnology rests on the conception of culture as an adaptive mechanism by which a certain number of human beings are enabled to live a social life as an ordered community in a given environment. Adaptation has two aspects, external and internal. The external aspect is seen in the relation of the society to its geographical environment. The internal aspect is seen in the controlled relations of individuals within the social unity. It is convenient to use the term "social integration" to cover all the phenomena of internal adaptation. One of the fundamental problems of a science of culture or of human society is therefore the problem of the nature of social integration.[36]

This is a clearer and more consistent statement than any offered by Malinowski, but once this tribute has been paid and its disciplinary value recognized, serious doubts arise. The "conception of culture as an adaptive mechanism" (he was to speak later of society as a natural organism) is a very limiting interpretation of French sociology and would appear to derive more from Herbert Spencer than from Durkheim. One may see an almost Benthamite connection in the development of the theory. Each society has its own system of moral customs; these are *explained* when it is seen how they serve to maintain the society in existence; that *explanation* is their social function. Analysis of these customs shows that they endorse and enforce certain values corresponding to social needs and these needs are basically related to the one social need, which is that for social integration.

The passage in which the above development occurs[37] is followed by argument deriving almost word for word from Durkheim's *Rules of Sociological Method*, although Durkheim himself is not mentioned. But the derivation is highly selective and significantly so. Despite the variations of different societies a certain system of sentiments and motives must exist in each individual mind and all have "a general substratum"; "there must be in the individual a strong feeling of attachment to his own group, to the social division ... to which he belongs." There must also be a sentiment of moral obligation, that some things must, and some things must not, be done. Finally, "perhaps less important, yet not less necessary there must be a sense of dependence on others, on society, tradition or custom." It is the way in which these and other sentiments work to maintain the cohesion of the society that Radcliffe-Brown calls their social function. These sentiments derive from an experience of a power outside the individual and this power is the "moral force of society". And this "moral force" comes to the individual in "definite concrete experiences only", that is, by interaction with others in some activity:

The Andaman Islander, like other savages,

the main concern of whose lives is the getting and eating of food, inevitably finds his experience of a moral force most intimately associated with the things he uses for food. Inevitably, therefore, he regards food as a substance in which, in some way, the moral force is inherent, since it is often through food that the force actually affects him and his actions.[38]

The moral force of society produces in the mind of the savage, since he cannot analyse it, "the more or less crude and undefined notion of a power in society and in nature having certain attributes". It is this power which is responsible for "all conditions of social euphoria or dysphoria". These collective sentiments are preserved in society and from generation to generation by being given regular and adequate expression. The social function of myths and rites is that they give verbal and physical expression to these sentiments.

Before considering the effects of this view of society it would be as well to note briefly the difference between it and that of Durkheim. The admittedly uneasy balance between collective representations and things in the latter's thought has disappeared. The "meaning" of any particular collective representation is reduced to the quality of a thing having value and function only in "the conception of culture as an adaptive mechanism". Secondly, the *sui generis* character of these collective representations is destroyed. Durkheim was explicit on this matter[39] and had said that once these collective representations existed they bore the same relation to their social substratum that the individual mind bore to its physical basis. They were not to be "explained" in terms of this or that particular characteristic of the social structure. This was, he said, most striking in the sphere of religion. And it was precisely because it was impossible to demonstrate the "immediate link" between the greater part of religious beliefs and social organizations that scholars had sought for "extra-sociological" causes in the formation of religions. By this way of argument, said Durkheim, one might as well eliminate from psychology anything which went beyond pure sensation. Third, and closely connected with the preceding, is the emphasis placed by Radcliffe-Brown upon the individual's "concrete experience" of interaction in society. Durkheim had certainly spoken and stressed the importance of what he called "the moments of social effervescence", when individuals come together and create or recreate their moral sense of society. This is for Durkheim a self-evident axiom of his sociology and in harmony with the analogy between society and the individual mind as regards their relations with their respective substrata. It does not play a great part in his discussion of actual phenomena and the manner in which collective representations are affirmed and reaffirmed is far from being "one of the fundamental problems of a science of culture", as Radcliffe-Brown supposed.

After Radcliffe-Brown social anthropology in England could only advance by rejecting his theories, not by developing them. It is therefore pertinent to ask why his theories should have had the effect they did, while more tentative and perceptive theoreticians were neglected. For judging by the works of this first generation of modern field-workers the speculations of Americans like Kroeber, Sorokin and Talcott Parsons are as if they had not been written, while the works of the Germans and the French were acceptable only as they were received from the hands of Radcliffe-Brown.

One can say at the outset that this apparently wanton disregard was born of a healthy empiricism. The followers of Malinowski and Radcliffe-Brown were not initially concerned with "society" but with this or that particular society, and these societies were relatively small preliterate ones. Any theory, to be acceptable to them, must prove its value in the description and analysis of these societies, while any attempt to offer a theory of "society" must wait upon the accumulation and classification of facts gathered in field-work. Malinowski had called for "a theory of a purely empirical nature" to meet the needs of modern field-work, "a theory which does not go beyond inductive evidence, but which provides for a clear understanding of how human culture, in its primitive form, works". Radcliffe-Brown's version of Durkheim met this need. For a generation dissatisfied with the piecemeal approach of the older ethnologists but at the same time unable to relate the speculative flights of sociologists to their own precise interests, Radcliffe-Brown provided the bridge. The conversion of ethnology into a branch of sociology had to take place first in the mind of an ethnologist. The revolution which took place in Radcliffe-Brown's mind is a sufficient contribution for one man to make and it is a lasting one.

Radcliffe-Brown's theories suited admirably the material of the earlier field-workers. The small societies which they studied were effectively united by the bonds of kinship and the natural boundaries of territory; the division of labour was seldom much advanced, if it was present at all; homogeneity of sentiment and occupation made analysis in terms of integration and permanence seem profitable. The unity of such societies was in fact the unity of kinsmen and groups of kin, and the question did not arise as to whether this was the only sociologically conceivable unity. During the period between the two world wars the contribution of English social anthropology to the subject as a whole was a large body of detailed facts about particular and unknown human societies studied as such and as fully as possible. It was in accordance with Radcliffe-Brown's empiricist emphasis that the greatest advance should have been in the fields of kinship, politics and law, for these were the spheres of human activity that were least distorted by the insistence upon "groups and relations between groups".

To draw attention, however, to the "somewhat narrow exegesis by Radcliffe-Brown of Durkheimian sociology"[40] is not merely an act of historical curiosity. It can be shown to have had, finally, a severely limiting effect upon social anthropology and given birth to conceptual distinctions which have occasionally degenerated into dogmas. The very nature of the societies studied under his influence precluded the inadequacies of his theory from being revealed, which is not surprising considering the circumstances of its genesis. But as a result two easy and interconnected assumptions came into being: firstly, that the theory accounted for all the facts of society, and secondly, that societies were indeed "adaptive mechanisms" to be defined on the basis of the physical interaction of individuals and groups.

For a generation of social anthropologists— mostly in England—the end of field-work seems to have been the search for the integrating factors in society, and this led them into circular arguments. Society is an adaptive mechanism and maintains its internal harmony as a natural organism is supposed to do. This harmony is demonstrated in the relationships between institutions and between these institutions and the general beliefs of the society; the function of the part is, then, its role in maintaining these relationships. As far as formal organization was concerned this function was given in the description of relationships—kinship maintained the solidarity of the clan, the chief became "a symbol of the solidarity of the tribe", the function of assemblies was to reaffirm the solidarity of those assembled. The problem came over those aspects of social life which were not immediately reducible to "groups and relations between groups" as Durkheim had noted. But the conception of society was not widened, as it had been by Durkheim. Instead, these phenomena were explained to the extent that they could be understood as integrative factors making for the integration of groups. Religion, various forms of art, including story-telling, dances and myths, the cosmologies of primitive peoples, could be shown to express, symbolize and stress certain values which were important to the continuance of the family or the tribe, and beyond that there was little to say about them. There was little to say about them because there was no language in which to say it. The business of social anthropology was the study of social structure and that was contained in the description of groups and relations between groups. Radcliffe-Brown's sociology provided no concepts, as Durkheim's had done, for the sociological consideration of these phenomena in their own right.

The most economical way of showing this inadequacy is to consider a brief and representative passage from one of Radcliffe-Brown's later

writings. The title—"Religion and Society"—
is immediately significant.[41] The political or
kinship system of a society is a system of
beliefs and actions no less than the religious
system, but no functionalist would have spoken
of kinship *and* society. Radcliffe-Brown begins
his discussion with the conventional statement
that all religions, or all except one, are usually
regarded as bodies of "illusory beliefs and illusory practices". We do not, he says, "believe
that the rain-making rites of savage tribes really
produce rain. Nor do we believe that the initi-
ates of the ancient mysteries did actually attain
through their initiation an immortality denied
to other men." If we adopt this point of view,
he continues, we are confronted with the "problem of how these beliefs came to be formulated
and accepted". This apparently direct approach
is not, he argues, the most profitable one as far
as understanding is concerned. The approach
which he proposes to adopt is not that of the
origins, but of the social functions, of religion.
The hypothesis would be that these functions
are independent of the truth or falsity of particular religions, which "may be important and
effective parts of the social machinery", and
that "without these 'false' religions social evolution and the development of modern civilization would have been impossible." In discussing this theory any anthropologist would agree
that in trying to understand a religion from the
sociological point of view its truth or falsity is
irrelevant. This is a recognition of mere fact,

for although one may know *what* someone believes one cannot know *how* someone believes without being that person. Even if one is interested in making a counter-statement of disbelief, this in turn is based upon certain beliefs, however unconscious they may be. But, in fact, despite Radcliffe-Brown's formal statement to the contrary, it is precisely his disbelief in what the primitive believes that is allowed to direct his study: "Without these 'false' religions social evolution ... would have been impossible." We note here the same uneasy movement between function and origin that we have seen in Durkheim's work; and it is significant. Although the intellectualist search for origins which might explain "how these beliefs came to be formulated and accepted" has been repudiated, the explanation of them in terms of function is still to explain *why* they continue to be accepted. This question, "Why?", limited only to a part of the phenomena manifested by a society, seems illegitimate. We could as well ask why a particular man believes that he has certain duties towards, and certain expectations from, his mother's brother. We may be able to say how or in what manner he conceives these rights and duties and we may see how they accord with other rights and duties in that society but if we ask why, the answer can only be: Because he has.

It is to this period that one can trace the opposition between society and culture which until very recently was considered useful.

Malinowski had not been over-concerned to imply any theoretical distinction in his use of these two words and even Radcliffe-Brown, in his earlier works, employed the word "culture" where later he would use the term "social structure". Once, however, the term "social structure" became common amongst anthropologists, with its narrow connotation of the social organization of groups, the term "culture" was left to cover those aspects of life not to be so described. With this a certain nationalism began to infect the subject as a whole.

Nothing has so far been said, apart from the mention of a few names, of the development of anthropology in America and Germany. A detailed consideration of the topic would call for more space than is available. The relation between the two countries is close, not least because of the German origin of Boas and many of the leading members of his school. It is also arguable that the German reaction in philosophy against the totalitarian aspect of Hegel's influence produced an equal tendency to view with suspicion the apparent totalitarianism of the Comtian tradition. The resultant emphasis upon the individual and his liberty might be related to the interest in psychological examination of social phenomena which I have already noted in Germany. Such a tradition would suit well with the preoccupations of an immigrant society concerned to weld into one nation individuals of very different social and racial backgrounds. It is perhaps significant that one of Boas's interests in the field of physical anthropology was to assess the changes in cranial measurement of second- and third-generation immigrants to the United States.

But whatever predispositions there may have been in America against the French sociological view of society, they were not weakened by that version of it which was offered in England. Before Radcliffe-Brown's views became current it is not easy to distinguish in the writings of American anthropologists any marked doctrinal bias which separates them from their English colleagues. As has been seen, the value of first-hand material had been appreciated early in the nineteenth century and had been reinforced by Boas's work. In the twentieth century there was, perhaps, a tendency to rely overmuch upon the field-work opportunities provided by the Indian reservations and to study these broken and often decimated groups as autonomous and untouched primitive societies. As compared with this, of course, the advantages provided for English anthropologists by British colonial interests were immense. But, with these differences, anthropologists in America and England, up to and including Malinowski, share a common tradition. After him, and increasingly, interests diverge so markedly as to threaten communication in some matters. In some quarters it is now accepted that the main anthropological interests in America and England, despite some individual instances to the contrary, are to be characterized as cultural and social anthropology respectively.

It is difficult to conceive what in thought or in fact this opposition of culture and society might correspond to. All one can do is to suggest the way in which it has developed, in the hope that a more critical examination will finally abandon it. The simplest form of the opposition is found in the aphorism of an American anthropologist: "Ants have society but men have culture", and in the use of the word "society" here I think it is possible to see the influence of, and reaction against, Radcliffe-Brown's terminology. In somewhat expanded form the distinction is well established by 1948. Herskovits, a senior American anthropologist, writes that a failure to distinguish the two terms "can seriously confuse our thinking":

> A culture is the way of life of a people; while a society is the organized aggregate of individuals who follow a given way of life. In still simpler terms a society is composed of people; the way they behave is their culture ... man shares with many other social animals the propensity to live in aggregates, but is the sole culture-building animal.[42]

This statement would appear to be a reintroduction of the much earlier distinction between natural (here social) and social (here cultural) man. But in effect, as the phrase "cultural anthropology" suggests, it may be better understood as a negative reaction to the narrowness of Radcliffe-Brown's conception of society. The implication is that if *social* anthropologists study social structure and if this structure is not conceptually distinct from the concrete organization of groups and their relationships, then it is the business of *cultural* anthropology to take cognizance of that mass of phenomena which are residual to that social structure.

The reaction had, historically, only a negative virtue. Radcliffe-Brown (following Durkheim in this) had integrated the observations of anthropologists within the world of sociological speculation, and any criticism of his views must grant that achievement. But this had not occurred in America. The older generation there clung to an *omnium-gatherum* view of man in society and continued to *explain* his activities partly in terms of supposed rational intentions, and the diffusion of culture traits, and survivals from the past; and, occasionally, in terms of psychological *meaning*. To the extent that observation was sensitively conducted, there was an increase in the knowledge of the range of human possibilities; but there was no development in theory. A younger generation, and especially those who had learnt the value of prolonged and intensive field-work in the Malinowskian manner, turned more to the characterization of cultures in psychological terms. This enterprise is notably associated with the name of Ruth Benedict, whose *Patterns of Culture* was published in 1934, and with

Margaret Mead, whose long succession of increasingly popular works has made her more representative of the subject in the public imagination than is entirely justified. But in general there was a movement in the 1930's and early 'forties in America towards the study of the individual in society. The emphasis was less upon society as such and more upon the individual's adaptation to, or reaction against, his society.

The need for field-work and the corresponding need for a sociological discipline tended to separate English anthropologists in the 'thirties from the speculations of their American colleagues. And in turn this very refusal of speculation became a closed system of thought. It is difficult to see how things could have been otherwise if the study of society was to advance in precision and subtlety. The English were increasingly concerned with the study of "primitive societies", and the realization that many of these were vanishing or being seriously modified by Western political dominance gave priority to the study of societies about which nothing was known. Each monograph, as it appeared, tended to deal with new problems. The intensive study of small tribes and peoples brought about an awareness in each worker of the immense complexity of social life, of the importance of the minutest detail, the significance of a certain intonation in speech or a certain gesture. Given this awareness it was difficult for them to see the relevance to their studies of the work of such distinguished scholars as Talcott Parsons in America, whose inadequacies at the empirical level preserved for him a certain catholicity of thought. Writing in 1937, Talcott Parsons criticized the " 'empiricist' conception of the relation between the theoretical system involved and concrete reality":

The effect of an empiricist position is to turn a logically closed into an empirically closed system. That is, in a logically closed system all the propositions in the system are, on the one hand, interdependent in that each has implications for the others and, on the other, the system is determinate in that each of these implications finds its statement in another proposition of the same system. But if this system alone is held to be adequate to the explanation of all the important concrete facts known about the phenomenon in question, then the propositions must include all these facts and their relations. In other words, empiricism transfers the logical determinism which is inherent in all scientific theory into an empirical determinism.[43]

This criticism, which today seems justified if applied to the later effects of Radcliffe-Brown's influence, went with, in the same work, a revaluation of Durkheim more subtle and profitable than anything that Radcliffe-Brown had offered in that connection. In its time it did not, however, have the same effect. It did not accord, as I have suggested, with the needs of field workers.

The empirical value of Radcliffe-Brown's work decreased as his statements about the nature of society become more dogmatic: societies were natural organisms and their study in terms of function and integration precluded the possibility of discussing the evident fact of change. The application of individual psychology to social phenomena was rightly rejected, but the individual, for whom words and actions have meaning, was eliminated with it; a natural science must not concern itself with speculative history and therefore history and the methods of historians were irrelevant. Empiricism became speculative in the worst sense and there was an evident need to return to the authority of human choice.

In effect a new approach was developing out of the increased emphasis upon field-work and it may be characterized as a shift from function to meaning. This shift and the attendant theoretical development are associated primarily with the works of E. E. Evans-Pritchard, who was to succeed Radcliffe-Brown in his chair at Oxford. In Professor Evans-Pritchard's first book, *Witchcraft, Oracles and Magic among the Azande*, published in 1937, there is no explicit expression of theoretical divergence, but in fact one hears little of the function of institutions. The phenomena under discussion are not *explained* solely by the extent to which they inspire and maintain sentiments which make for the integration of Zande society. The concern is rather to show first what the Azande do and what they believe about their actions, and then to relate beliefs and actions to each other in such a manner that, given certain premises, they are seen to constitute a logical system. Secondly, this system is related to, and seen to be in meaningful accord with, the formal social organization of the Azande and with the general view that they have of the universe in which they live. Neither from the facts adduced nor from the manner in which they are explained would it be possible to extract anything resembling a law of human society or even a scientific statement about witchcraft in general. The analysis goes through the distinctive appearances of Zande magic to find out what the Azande have in common with other societies. There emerges an implicit comparison between their witchcraft and our notions of belief, causality and moral system, and also a heightened consciousness of what we ourselves mean by these terms. This implicit comparison becomes explicit when we pass to the study of another society. It is important to note that by this stage the individual institution—in this case, witchcraft—is only the point of entry to the perception of sets of relations. In short, one can begin to speak of the structural analysis of social life as opposed to the functional analysis of social structures.

This advance is even more apparent in a slightly later work, *The Nuer* (1940). This book, which is concerned with "the modes of livelihood and political institutions of a Nilotic people", might well by its subject have been an essay in the study of integration and its divergence (again largely implicit) from any such theory is all the more interesting. The apparent anarchy of Nuer life and the bewildering series of allegiances according to which they act in varying circumstances are not in fact rendered intelligible by an hypostatization of the groups between which relationships are observed. At the end of his concluding summary the author writes:

> Social anthropology deals at present in crude concepts, tribe, clan, age-set, &c., representing social masses and a supposed relation between these masses. The science will make little progress on this low level of abstraction, if it be considered abstraction at all, and it is necessary for further advance to use the concepts to denote relations, defined in terms of social situations, and relations between these relations.[44]

The enquiry works through the relativities of Nuer language so that what is meaningful and therefore systematic to the Nuer becomes meaningful and systematic for the observer. An example taken from the book itself relates to the discussion of the Nuer word which may be translated "home". There is a refusal to define the term as having one correct meaning and referent to which other meanings are secondary. Rather the word is defined in terms of "the relativity of the group values to which it refers":

> If one meets an Englishman in Germany, and asks him where his home is, he may reply that it is in England. If one meets the same man in London and asks him the same question he will tell one that his home is in Oxfordshire, whereas if one meets him in that county he will tell one the name of the town or village in which he lives.[45]

The fact that the analysis is conducted in the realization that the words used and the things or behaviour to which they refer are to be understood in their relatedness as constituting meaningful systems—this is what marks the originality of *The Nuer*. Since Malinowski, social anthropologists had laid great stress upon the importance of learning the language of the people studied. Now the social aspect of language became a clue to a new kind of analysis. Following the passage quoted, Professor Evans-Pritchard continues:

> I emphasize this character of structural distance at an early stage because an understanding of it is necessary to follow the account of various social groups which we are about to describe. Once it is understood the apparent contradictions in our account

will be seen to be contradictions in the structure itself, *being, in fact, a quality of it.*[46]*

The analysis results in a statement of Nuer political life in terms of complementary tendencies towards fission and fusion which is called the "segmentary principle". This is arrived at through, and in turn renders intelligible, not only the political behaviour of these people but also their concepts of time and space and the relationships which they maintain with their habitat. The contradiction which is a quality of the structure is thus represented as a relation of opposition in the final account and a kind of thinking which is markedly dialectical takes the place of a language imitating the general propositions of natural science.

To enforce the importance of this movement from function to meaning and to draw attention to an independent development along the same lines in France, the following remarks by Professor Lévi-Strauss, written in 1950, are of great value:

It is in this relational character of symbolic thought that we can find the answer to our problem. Whatever may have been the moment and the circumstances of its appearance in the scale of animal life, language could only have been born at once in its entirety. Things are not able to come to have meaning progressively. At the end of a transformation to be studied not by the social

* My italics.

sciences but by biology and psychology, a movement was effected from a stage where nothing had meaning to another where everything had it. This apparently commonplace remark is important because this radical change is without a counterpart in the field of knowledge which does develop slowly and progressively. Put another way, from the moment when the entire Universe became, at one stroke, significant, it was not for all that better known, even if it is true that the appearance of language precipitated the rhythm of the development of knowledge.[47]

Since there is some indication that the full implications of this movement from function to meaning were not drawn by all social anthropologists in the post-war period it is important to distinguish Evans-Pritchard's analysis from what Radcliffe-Brown had, in 1930, called the "law of opposition".* He had defined it as follows:

> In any segmentary organization the unity and solidarity of a group or segment depends upon the existence of some form of social opposition, i.e., some form of socially regulated and organized antagonism, between it

* Cited by M. N. Srinivas in *Method in Social Anthropology* (selected essays, ed. Srinivas, Chicago, 1958). Four years before his death in 1955 he was to use the term "opposition"—"that universal feature of human thinking"—in a sense quite different to the above. But there is no sign that he was aware of a radical departure from a previous position. See Srinivas, p. 118.

and the other groups or segments with which it is in contact, which opposition serves to keep the separate segments differentiated and distinct. Opposition, which I am here using as a technical term for socialized or institutionalized antagonism, may take many different forms, and warfare is only one of them.

It is evident that here the term "opposition" is being used in a limited and indeed rather obvious sense, and even in this sense it is not entirely correct. Even if we accept the emphasis upon the solidarity of "the group" it is not the case that a sense of identity is always preserved by some form of antagonism. Quite distinct is the use of the term "opposition" in the phrase "complementary opposition". I need not, incidentally, go into the question as to how, in Radcliffe-Brown's conception, a natural organism could be divided by internal antagonisms.

The way in which Professor Evans-Pritchard handles his material is incompatible with any sociology deriving from Spencer. It is possible, on the other hand, to relate it to the French school, and even earlier it finds an echo in the commonsensical reaction of Adam Ferguson to the dogmatic speculation of his own time:

The titles of *fellow citizen* and *countryman* unopposed to those of *alien* and *foreigner*, to which they refer, would fall into disuse, and lose their meaning.[48]

The author's refusal to make explicit the shift in emphasis had certain tactical advantages. No storm blew up which might have obscured the presentation under a cloud of dust, a sense of continuity was preserved and many younger anthropologists were able to see the deeper relevance of language to their studies. It was no longer satisfying to assume that a given group of people came together to "affirm their solidarity" once it became evident that the people themselves did not think so. The reason for their coming together must be the reason they gave and this must be the anthropologist's starting point.

But there were temporary disadvantages also in the implicitness of this return to the authority of human choice. The moral content of the old image of society remained. Despite the fact that even one man or one group in a particular society was seen to be subject to contradictory motives and conflicting interests, finally the theoretical concern of the anthropologist was to discover beneath everything not merely regularities but harmony; society, a natural organism, by its nature resolved all difficulties and survived, however unconsciously, as the highest good.

But historically it seems unlikely that this situation might have been prevented by an earlier formal definition of position. When later, in 1950, Professor Evans-Pritchard explicitly rejected the claim of social anthropology as a natural science, his dereliction was criticized by those who had never hesitated to praise the quality of his field analyses.[49]

A brief example of the survival into the post-war period of the harmonious society preserving its solidarity is contained in a small popular book by Professor M. Gluckman. Here material from various parts of Africa, including the Zande and Nuer, is brought together to show

> ... that conflicts in one set of relationships, over a wider range of society or through a longer period of time, lead to the re-establishment of social cohesion ... I shall exhibit this process through the working of the feud, of hostility to authority, of estrangements within the elementary family, of witchcraft accusations and ritual and even in the colour-bar.[50]

Here the two senses of the word "opposition" are used interchangeably. To say that a given group defines itself, can only be said to exist, in opposition to another, is not to say that these groups are necessarily in conflict. On the other hand, two conflicting groups with a common goal, as in our Wars of the Roses, may be said, imaginatively, to be "united in the strife which divided them",* but it is only imaginatively

---

* This, from T. S. Eliot's *Little Gidding*, is not a mere adorn ment to my page. Mr Eliot later translated this striking phrase into prose and offered it as part of his *Notes Toward the Definition of Culture*, a book cited by Professor Gluckman as an authority.

effective when the goal is of its nature indivisible and this is so in very particular circumstances. The Lion and the Unicorn are united in their interest in the Crown but they do not affirm their solidarity, they do not cohere and when they come to plum-cake, they divide it. To sum up with a brief example: a definition of the phrase "British constitution" would involve an account of the formal opposition of Monarch and Parliament, Lords and Commons, of Government and Opposition. Each opposition is in fact pointed by acts and conventional phrases which symbolize the opposition. These acts and phrases appear to have their origin in particular historical conflicts but they are not conflicts nor do they entail conflict. Actual antagonism can occur and indeed does occur but it is in particular circumstances and what it not surprisingly brings about is something resembling organic unity within the opposed parties or factions.

The difficulty inherent in his approach is finally demonstrated by Gluckman in his last chapter. Following his dialectical rhythm ("The Peace in the Feud", "The License in Ritual") it is entitled "The Bonds in the Colour Bar". Here, apart from the evident fact that an understanding of South African society must take account of the colour-bar, one might expect to find that racial discrimination, "over a wider range of society or through a longer period of time, lead[s] to the re-establishment of social cohesion". This is so obviously unshowable that finally the attempt to resolve thesis and antithesis in terms of the thesis breaks down.

I do not propose to consider in any detail the developments in social anthropology after the Second World War. One would be involved in personalities and the nuances of difference which inevitably appear as one comes closer to one's own time. I have characterized the contribution of Evans-Pritchard as the return to meaning from function and although, as we have seen, the implications of this have not been fully or universally accepted, an increasingly authoritative body of scholars is proving the value of this redirection. In France Claude Lévi-Strauss, by emphasizing the relation in method between social anthropology and linguistics or theories of communication has, perhaps more explicitly than anyone, drawn the line between the definition of the sociologist's position and the definition of his object. The preoccupation with the latter marks the would-be natural scientist in our studies, while a concern with the former remains prerequisite if we are to discuss social phenomena scientifically. Lévi-Strauss has shown that we do not need to limit ourselves to this or that definition of society, which inevitably brings about such divisions as that between society and culture; on the other hand, the attempt to match the relatedness of social phenomena with a relational analysis, a structural approach, has proved its value by presenting systematic explanations of apparently diverse phenomena without subtracting the diversity.*

III

In this concluding section I propose to abandon the attempt to give an account of the development of social anthropology and to return to the consideration of two problems which have been constantly in the air throughout the preceding pages—the problem of objectivity and the problem of comparison. We have seen that the first important step was the reintegration of society in nature but that from the English empiricists a line runs through Spencer to Radcliffe-Brown which increasingly stresses not only the view that societies are natural systems, but that they must be studied by a natural science in the hope of finding laws comparable with those of the natural sciences. The empirical tradition becomes empiricist and, in effect, more and more speculative. As it becomes speculative its moral

* See, for example, his "Le Dédoublement de la représentation dans les arts de l'Asie et de l'Amérique", republished in his collected essays, *Anthropologie structurale*, Paris, Plon, 1958. I would refer the reader also to the translation of a piece of work by L. Dumont, "A Structural Definition of a Folk Deity", in *Contributions to Indian Sociology*, vol. 3 (1959). The clarity and economy of this latter essay shows that social anthropology, like mathematics, is not without its own aesthetic.

assumptions become more blatant and (though in a very different form) there emerges a picture of society not unlike that against which Hume and his school were fighting. If societies are natural systems maintaining their internal harmony, everything that happens in social life is natural, is inevitable, and cannot but be accepted as good. Because, also, the sociologist can only talk about man inasmuch as he thinks and acts in society, the observations of the sociologist, no less than the myths of the primitive he studies, are determined by his own society, by his own class, by his own intellectual environment. In short, the more he strives to achieve what he believes to be the objectivity of natural science, the more he falls into moral relativity and solipsism. It is essential, then, to consider what the word "objectivity" can mean to a social anthropologist in relation to the work he does.

It is evident at the outset that the anthropologist working in another society (or in his own society regarded as "other") must take a certain stance quite different from that of, say, a government official or missionary, who is concerned to bring about change in accordance with certain beliefs which he holds.* The

* It would be elaborating the obvious to argue at length that the government official and the missionary are more effective in their work to the extent that they take cognizance of the anthropologist's findings. What does need to be stressed for the sake of what follows is that anthropology does not destroy the grounds of action, provided that it steers clear of solipsist assumptions.

anthropologist is concerned with a systematic understanding of what he sees going on around him. He learns the culture, as he learns the language of the people, on the assumption that action and belief are no more random than language. The first step is to find out by participation and identification the meaning which people themselves attach to what they do. He does not assume at the outset that phenomena may be labelled political, religious or economic because that is what initially they mean to him. To do so would be like discovering some dangerous sect of anarchists in the suburbs of an English city that deliberately exploited the Christian Sunday in order to endanger their neighbours' fences, and obscure visibility for traffic, by lighting large (possibly sacrificial) fires at the bottoms of their gardens. The anthropologist, by not assuming that what he sees he immediately understands, places himself "outside" the society he studies and to this extent he approaches social facts "as though they were things". But (and here a distinction between what is evident to the senses and what is meaningful is relevant) he is obliged by the very terms of his first objective stance to enter into his object, because the object is, unlike a natural organism, one into which he can enter. "Things" cannot remain meaningless to him, and just as, and to the extent that, he becomes conscious and rejects his subjective interpretation, he is obliged to accept the interpretation offered by others—here the people who do, see, use and value "things". The anthropologist, if he were to do only this but do it well, could still only claim to be a journalist, at best an artist. But he does not stop there. Professor Lévi-Strauss has discussed this matter with great clarity. The business of the anthropologist is to construct models which are quite distinct and not to be reduced to the observable social relationships in a given society.

> Is there not a contradiction between ethnographic observation, always concrete and individualized, and structural research which often appears to have a formal and abstract character? ... From my point of view ... there is no contradiction but an intimate correlation between the concern for concrete detail distinctive of the ethnographic description, and the validity and generality which I claim for the model constructed upon it.[51]

He goes on to say that various serviceable models could be constructed to explain one group of phenomena:

> Nevertheless, the best will always be the *true* model, that is to say the one which, while being the most simple, answers the two conditions of not using facts other than those considered and giving an account of all of them.[52]

Characteristically giving credit to Boas for the distinction, he then discusses conscious and unconscious models. Simplifying his argument, one could say that the conscious model is the meaning which people themselves attach to their behaviour to the extent that they have even a rudimentary notion of its ideal form. Such would be a diagram scratched in the sand by a Nuer trying to explain his relation to his own or another lineage. The unconscious model is the grammar of a language, the structure of a society, which on occasion may diverge markedly from the ideal picture which the people themselves present. "There are", says Lévi-Strauss, "two reasons why we should respect these 'home-made' conscious models":

> First they may be good, or at least may offer a point of access to the structure; each culture has its theoreticians, whose work merits as much attention as does that of the ethnologist's colleagues. Next, even if these models are tendentious or inexact, the tendency and the kind of error which they reveal are an integral part of the facts to be studied; and perhaps they may be counted amongst the most significant of these ...
>
> Durkheim and Mauss well understood that the conscious representations of the indigenous people were always worth more attention than the theories issuing—equally as conscious representations—from the observer's society.[53]

But finally, once the priority of the indigenous meaning has been granted, the social anthropologist moves from art towards science to the extent that he recognizes that this meaning is only a part, however essential, of the totality which he is concerned to explain. This needs to be stressed, for there are still those for whom there is no scientific alternative between natural science and art. In another context, Professor Lévi-Strauss criticizes Mauss for adducing ideas of secret power and mysterious force as part of a sociological analysis of magic and thus limiting himself to the indigenous model.

> But these notions of sentiment, of the fortuitous and arbitrary, are not scientific notions. They throw no light on the phenomena which it is proposed to explain, they participate in them.[54]

In short, the work of the social anthropologist may be regarded as a highly complex act of translation in which author and translator collaborate. A more precise analogy is that of the relation between the psychoanalyst and his subject. The analyst enters the private world of his subject in order to learn the grammar of his private language. If the analysis goes no further it is no different in kind from the understanding which may exist between any two people who know each other well. It becomes scientific to the extent that the private language of intimate understanding is translated into a public language, however specialized from the layman's point of view, which in this case is the language of psychologists. But the particular act of translation does not distort the private experience of the subject and ideally it is, at least potentially, acceptable to him as a scientific representation of it. Similarly, the model of Nuer political life which emerges in Professor Evans-Pritchard's work is a scientific model meaningful to his fellow-sociologists as sociologists, and it is effective because it is potentially acceptable to the Nuer in some ideal situation in which they could be supposed to be interested in themselves as men living in society. The collaboration of natural scientists may from this point of view be seen as a developing language enabling certain people to communicate with increasing subtlety about a distinct area of natural phenomena which is defined by the name of the particular science. Their science is, in the literal meaning of the term, their common sense, their common meaning. To move from this common sense to the "common sense" of the wider public involves again an act of translation. The situation of social anthropology, or sociology in general, is not at this level so very different. The difference lies in the fact that sociological phenomena are objectively studied only to the extent that their subjective meaning is taken into account and that the people studied are potentially capable of sharing the sociological consciousness that the sociologist has of them.

Clearly this argument for sociology as a science is concerned only with the actual operations of science. The relation between observer and observed and between the observers is the important one. The ends of particular sciences, the nature of their generalizations, their use or lack of use for particular purposes, are various and secondary.

For the "natural scientists" of society the goal after the accumulation of a sufficient number of facts was definition, comparison and classification. Social anthropologists continue to-day to speak of the desirability of comparative studies, but formally little is done in this direction. Informally, comparison is built into the method of the subject, for even in his first piece of field-work the anthropologist is comparing the categories of his own society with those of the society he studies; he has in mind also the works of his predecessors which deal with phenomena similar to those that he finds. This implicit comparison is instructive, for it suggests a kind of more formal comparison quite different from that envisaged by Radcliffe-Brown. The field-worker in a given society starts off with the experience of difference and as he learns the culture of his people and compares it with his own or that of others he discovers very simple similarities. But these similarities enable him to see all the more clearly the significant differences, which in turn again make way for a deeper apprehension of similarities. This process is constant to such an extent that one might say that social anthropology is of its nature comparative.

More formal comparison is both possible and

desirable, but here again the concern will be not with similarities only, for the sake of some pseudo-biological classification, but with differences also, for the sake of heightened understanding. Once social phenomena are recognized to be collective representations as well as things it is difficult to see what objective criteria could provide the base of a typology or, indeed, what purpose such a typology could serve. The dangers of such classifications, and the inevitable definitions that precede them, may be seen from a particular case. Among the Nilotic peoples, of whom the Nuer are one, there are, amongst others, two with very marked superficial differences of political institutions—the Shilluk and the Anuak.[55] The former people have a centralized polity and a king; the latter have a highly complex organization centring upon certain emblems which imply or symbolize kingship and confer nobility upon the holder, but there is no king. The Nuer have no such centralizing institution. Were we to attempt the classifications of these peoples in terms of the apparently convenient distinction between centralized and acephalous polities, it is evident that the Nuer would fall into one class and the Shilluk into another. The Anuak would fall into a sub-class of either type with equal convincingness. But to arrive at this classification we should have had to abstract all that these three peoples have quite obviously in common—cultural characteristics, quite apart from linguistic ones, which justify us in the first place in speaking of them all as Nilotic. If, on the other hand, we refuse either the similarities or differences of abstracted institutions we can perceive a structure basic to all three.

Towards the end of his account of the Nuer Professor Evans-Pritchard speaks of individuals in recent Nuer history whom he calls prophets and in a later work compares with the Nuer priests as follows:

> The priest is a traditional functionary ... the prophet is a recent development. The priest has an appointed sacrificial role in certain situations ... the prophet's functions are indeterminate. The priest's powers are transmitted by descent ... the prophet's powers are charismatic—an individual inspiration. The virtue of the priest resides in his office; that of the prophet in himself. The priest has no cult; the prophet has certain cultic features. But the most outstanding conceptual difference is that whereas in the priest man speaks to God, in the prophet God, in one of his hypostases, speaks to man. The priest stands on the earth and looks to the sky. Heavenly beings descend from the sky and fill the prophets.[56]

The Nuer clearly distinguish between these two but have no idea of hostility between them; indeed one and the same man may be both priest and prophet. To be a prophet is not the ambition of the average Nuer, it results from a literally eccentric act of will:

> There is nothing an ordinary Nuer desires less
> than to be in contact with Spirit. He seeks
> by sacrifice to rid himself of it or to keep it
> at a distance, for it is dangerous to him. But
> a prophet sought inspiration, entry of Spirit
> into himself ...[57]

The apparently recent (1906) emergence of
these figures coincides with the impact upon
Nuer society of Arab and European aggression.
More generally, they were associated with war-
fare and with raids upon the neighbouring
Dinka people:

> For the first time a single person symbolized,
> if only to a moderate degree and in a mainly
> spiritual and uninstitutionalized form, the
> unity of a tribe, for prophets are tribal figures.
> But they have a further significance, for their
> influence extended over tribal boundaries. ...
> They were ... pivots of federation between
> adjacent tribes and personified the structural
> principle of opposition in its widest expres-
> sion, the unity and homogeneity of Nuer
> against foreigners.[58]

The author goes on to suggest that since the
Sky Spirit tended to possess the son of the
prophet on his death there is some evidence
that a hereditary politico-religious leadership
might, but for the victory and interference of
the British Government, have emerged.

Whatever the particular historical circumstances of this emergence it is not "explained"
by them. Professor Evans-Pritchard insists:

The rise of prophets ... may indeed be a
response first to a challenge and then to disintegration, but it is a response made within
a set of religious conceptions and has, therefore, a significance for a study of those conceptions without regard to whatever it may
have been which occasioned the response.[59]

In other words the segmentary principle of
fission and fusion which characterized the
structural analysis of Nuer political life is seen
to operate, not surprisingly, in their religious
life. The emergence of a sole religious figure to
symbolize political unity is not an accident or a
freak of chance, but an event entirely in accordance with the basic principles by which Nuer
life can be seen as a systematic whole.

I shall return to this example for another and
connected purpose. All I am concerned to show
at the moment is that if we rise above the concrete appearances and compare politico-religious relations among the three Nilotic peoples
I have mentioned, we discover a basic similarity which corresponds to the facts and at the
same time enables us to proceed to a more dis-
criminating analysis of the differences in which,
after all, their distinctive individualities lie.
This, I suggest, is a sociological comparison,
even if it is a simple one. It has this to be said
for it, that the terms to be compared derive
from the facts themselves, and are not arbitrar-
ily imposed upon the material by an assumption
that what we ourselves verbally oppose (cen-

tralized and non-centralized) is necessarily and universally a significant opposition in social life.

For Radcliffe-Brown and for a few social anthropologists today, comparison should lead to the formulation and validation of "statements about the conditions of existence of social systems (laws of social statics) and the regularities that are observable in social change (laws of social dynamics)".[60] It is a comparison seeking for what is common in societies all over the world; the items compared are the lowest common denominators of man's social life, and the laws which are to result are inevitably platitudes.

There remain three problems which have been adverted to but not dealt with in the preceding pages: the position of the individual, the nature of social change, the place of history. I propose to suggest that in fact these are all aspects of one problem which could only emerge for consideration once social anthropologists had rejected the dogmatic adherence to natural science.

In 1951 Radcliffe-Brown wrote:

Anthropology, as the study of primitive societies, includes both historical ... studies and also the generalizing study known as social anthropology which is a special branch of comparative sociology. It is desirable that the aims and methods should be distinguished ... it is for this reason that thirty years ago I urged that there should be a clear distinction between ethnology as the historical study of primitive societies and social anthropology. ... We can leave all questions of historical reconstruction to ethnology. For social anthropology the task is to formulate and validate statements about the conditions of existence of social systems (laws of social statics) and the regularities that are observable in social change (laws of social dynamics). This can only be done by the systematic use of the comparative method.[61]

The view of an alternative use of comparison presented earlier, comparison concerned with similarities and differences, brings about a view of society and the study of society quite contrary to the one implied above. Social anthropology is not divided from history as a generalizing study is divided from a particularizing one. Social anthropology is no less concerned with individuals than history, while no modern historian can afford to neglect the social component of the individual people or events that he studies. The difference is not in the object of study; it is not the difference between the study of the past and the study of the present. The difference is in the stress laid by either discipline upon different relations. The historian is concerned with the relations between individuals (individual people, groups, or events) that produce change; the social anthropologist has been concerned so far more with the

atemporal patterns by which a society can be
seen as a meaningful whole. It is not my business to suggest to historians that the study of
some existing polities in Africa might deepen
their understanding of past political events.
Rather, I would suggest in this context that the
social anthropologist has to modify his picture
of society in such a manner that it is seen to
exist, as indeed it does exist, in time. In other
words, he has to come closer to the reality in
his conceptualization of it without, for all that,
turning into a historian. The relation between
history and sociology cannot be conceived in
the terms suggested by Radcliffe-Brown. To
take a concrete instance, Professor Evans-
Pritchard reinforces his analysis of the Nuer
political life which he observed by taking cognizance of individual phenomena, the historical
emergence of the prophets. These were regarded as individual events and individual
eccentrics by the Nuer themselves, but he himself had not observed them. And only by seeing
Nuer society both statically and in time—as
having, that is to say, certain individual poten-
tialities which are not constantly manifest—
can we effect a true comparison of it with other
Nilotic societies.

The model of society which needs to be
modified is the one inherited from Durkheim.
We may and do approach society as a *sui-
generis* synthesis, as if it were more than the
sum of its parts, but it has become all too easy
to pass from an assumption made for the

purposes of analysis to a statement about the nature of the phenomena studied. This passage is almost inevitable, however, for the original assumption lays its sole emphasis upon aggregation and permanence in such a manner that there is no language in which to describe the relation of the aggregate to the individuals composing it or the relation of this permanence to change. In short what is lacking is a recognition of the *principium individuationis* as a principle, however paradoxical it may seem, in social life.

If the theory we have divides what is not divided in human experience we must return to that experience, to the common sense, in order to rectify it. We say that primitive or traditional societies change so slowly that for all practical intents and purposes they may be discussed as unchanging. We contrast them with our own society, which, we say, is rapidly changing. When do we experience this rapid change? It is not the case that we get up each morning, make a rapid assessment of our new identity and then cautiously approach our acquaintance to discover if they have changed as much as or more than we have. And yet we know that we and the relationships we maintain are subject to duration. Conversely, it is only to think of the Nuer as human beings to recognize that they cannot be without an experience of the changes that are brought about by duration. All men die, but this man has not died before. The unique experience which individual people have of individual events is a fact of human life that is not explained away by the general and atemporal propositions which render it meaningful (usually in religious terms) to the people themselves. Even less is it to be explained away or disregarded by general and atemporal propositions formulated by sociologists. Both we and the Nuer as individuals constantly experience the individuality of other individual people and groups, perform and suffer constantly individual and unique events. We both continue nevertheless to use the words of yesterday for the meanings of today and to act as though our relationships with others did not change. In short, if we submit the saying of Heraclitus to the test of our own experience, we may know that we do not step into the same river twice and yet we act, and must act, as if we did.

The relevance of this apparent contradiction to our study of society is one of the preoccupations in the work of Ernst Cassirer:

In all human activities we find a fundamental polarity, which may be described in various ways. We may speak of a tension between stabilization and evolution, between a tendency that leads to fixed stable forms of life and another tendency to break up this rigid scheme. ... There is a ceaseless struggle between tradition and innovation, between reproductive and creative forces. This dualism is to be found in all the domains of cultural life. What varies is the proportions of the opposing factors. Now the one factor, now the other, seems to preponderate. This preponderance to a high degree determines the character of the single forms and gives to each of them its particular physiognomy.[62]

Cassirer goes on to present this dialectic in some wider evolutionary scale as far as religious life is concerned. Here we must part company with him, if only to draw attention to his real contribution. If, as he says, in myth and in primitive religion the tendency to stabilization is so strong that it entirely outweighs the opposite pole, the dialectic is effectually destroyed and the Nuer, for example, are to be denied, what is undeniable, the individual's experience of individual events. It is equally impossible to accept that in modern society the balance falls so unequivocally upon the side of the individual. This would be to affirm in one sphere of social life what is denied in others and flatly contradicts Cassirer's concern to demonstrate the homogeneity of cultural life. We can see here, incidentally, that a concern with human activity or cultural life without an informing sociological preoccupation leads to the kind of statement that the field-work of the thirties factually disproved.

It is when he turns to language that the force of Cassirer's argument becomes clearer, though even here we have to note a certain failure to argue from human experience in society as it is. "Language", he says, "is one of the firmest conservative powers in human culture."

Without this conservatism it could not fulfil its principal task, communication. Communication requires strict rules. Linguistic symbols and forms must have a stability and constancy in order to resist the dissolving and destructive influence of time. Nevertheless phonetic change and semantic change are not only accidental features in the development of language. They are inherent and necessary conditions of this development.[63]

But the conservatism of language over against the "dissolving and destructive influence of time" is secondary to its daily function in any society, which is to conserve meaning "in order to resist the dissolving and destructive influence" of the individual's experience. For it is a platitude that to the extent that experience is individual experience it cannot be communicated, and it is equally evident that there can be no communication without individuals with experience to communicate. If it were possible for the individual to communicate the totality of his individual experience he would cease to exist as an individual; if, on the other hand, the individuality of his experience is stressed at the expense of communication there can, ultimately, be no communication at all. These truisms, which we accept in our appreciations of literature, painting and the arts generally, and in our assessments of individual artists, only need to be extended and generalized for a model of society to emerge which loses nothing in analytical rigour and has the virtue of being grounded in experience. If this does not happen, we separate off a part only of our own social experience, that which makes for stability, and project it upon the societies that we study.

Social change and the place of historical evidence are, then, aspects of the problem of the individual in that wider sense of the word which embraces people, groups and events, — the *principium individuationis*. In our day-to-day life the interplay of our individuality and our sociality is constant. We know that we are subject to duration, we know equally that in order to act meaningfully (which includes communication) we must assume the contrary. In communication itself, however elaborate and profound the attempt to communicate may be, there is the residuum of experience which is individual, which is not communicated but which provides the necessary ground of any communication. The events, petty or major, which occur are, simply by their occurrence in duration, unique: the primitive may render them meaningful to himself in terms of some mythic charter or some cosmic struggle,[64] we no less render them meaningful to ourselves in terms of the order in which we live and against which only they are seen as events.

There is a pragmatic tradition in social

anthropology, strongly connected with the field-work tradition, that subjects propositions to the test of usefulness in the field. I have suggested, for instance, that writers of the intellectual distinction of Cassirer were ignored because they did not appear to answer the questions which field-workers had to ask. In the present context it could be suggested that this general view of society as a dialectical process between the principles making for individuation and the principles making for aggregation is an unnecessary refinement. For it is the case that the traditionalist societies that we study do appear to lay stress less upon the individual, and value change less, than we do. Is it then so unreasonable to accept as a "working hypothesis" the picture of these societies as unchanging? It is unreasonable for a variety of reasons. Factually, there are very few societies left in the world which have not entered the orbit of our industrial civilization. If the anthropologist abstracts the society he is studying from this orbit he is violating his material. Secondly, if he wishes to study a changing society the language of functionalism does not enable him to do so. Since he conceives society atemporally the discussion of social change is reduced to a descriptive comparison of the society "then" and the society "now", effectively, in the functionalist conception, two qualitatively different societies. Even for such comparison he has no terms once the mere tabulation of apparently similar characteristics

has been abandoned as unsatisfactory. Indeed, it is in comparison that recognizes the
importance of difference that the value of the
principle of individuation as between two
societies, is most apparent. Finally, this "working hypothesis" is no such thing but only an
unexamined assumption similar to the assumptions concerning meaning and communication
in daily life in society. One could go so far as to
adapt Lévi-Strauss's judgement and say that it
is an assumption which does not clarify the
operations of collective representations, it only
participates in them.

At this stage it is advisable to point out that
what is being offered here is not a new theory,
which would be out of place in a general
account of the subject. It is, however, an
attempt to draw a little more fully the implications of the emphasis, born of experience in the
field, upon meaning. The concern with function was, however inaccurate, a concern which
could be called scientific. The new emphasis
upon meaning could, given the irreducible
individualities of the various kinds of society
in the world, place the anthropologist in a
predicament belonging to the experience of art.
The further he goes in communicating the
experience he has of a particular society the
more he feels that he is departing from the
experience which that society has, in a manner
of speaking, of itself. Practically, this has been
recognized by many anthropologists, who avoid
direct translation of indigenous terms and

prefer to signify their meanings by description of the various contexts in which they are used. But obviously the ideal monograph along these lines would be written entirely in the indigenous language; the situation would be analogous to that of a poet trying to communicate in a language invented by himself and there could in fact be no sociology. It is by recognizing that he is engaged in a dialogue of three—himself, the society studied and his fellow sociologists—that the objectivity peculiar to his work is preserved and can claim scientific precision. It is clear that if he eliminates any of the partners in this dialogue—that is to say, if he denies the individuality of the society studied, of his own experience of it, or of sociology as a particular discipline—the dialogue is broken and he falls back into the collective representations of his own or of the other society.

When we turn from what many anthropologists say that they are doing to what in fact they do, the gulf between what has here been formally stated and the work actually done is considerably decreased. The increasing emphasis laid in the last few years by Professors Evans-Pritchard and Lévi-Strauss upon history and language has not been welcomed by many of their colleagues, who continue nevertheless to admire the precise application of their theories in particular analyses. One could go further, and show that implicitly the work of several formal adherents of Radcliffe-Brownian sociology succeed to the extent that they depart from it along the lines indicated here. One example must suffice.

One of the major themes of Professor M. Gluckman's study of *The Judicial Process Among the Barotse of Northern Rhodesia* develops as follows. Many of the legal rules are found to be general—as, for example, "A husband must treat his wife properly and care for her."

> The rule has definite meaning but it has to be *specified*, by being applied in a variety of specific situations to particular circumstances. Since the standard in any such situation is ... "an upright husband", the judges are able to specify the rule in terms of current as well as traditional usage.[65]

Barotse life has changed under British rule, missionary activity has changed the moral ambience, new forms of property have emerged. Nevertheless:

> The central rule, "a husband must treat his wife properly and care for her", has persisted from before British occupation until to-day. The specification or definition, of "the upright husband" ... has altered to absorb these changes in social life. ... The concepts are ... *flexible*: more specifically they are *elastic*, in that they can be stretched to cover new types of behaviour, new institutions, new customs. ... This flexibility is a characteristic of all legal concepts.[66]

The Lozi, the ruling people of Barotseland, distinguish between law and facts but the distinction has not been hardened into one which binds the judges. New situations are dealt with according to traditional maxims and the traditional maxims are in turn modified.

> Clearly they occasionally, unconsciously as well as consciously, develop the law to create new legal rules and sanctions in order to meet situations which they define as unprecedented. [But] ... This creation of new rules should be made within the framework of Lozi law.[67]

The problem, for the author, emerges then as follows. The general concepts or maxims have meanings, but these are wide and general enough to cover a variety of cases. They are at the same time precise in their application; that is to say, precise decisions are rendered in terms of them.

> They are both "certain" and "uncertain" ... I hope to resolve this paradox by showing how it lies at the root of the Lozi judicial process, so that the "uncertainty" of legal concepts has social value in maintaining the certainty of law.[68]

Almost from the very words used here we can see a preoccupation very close to that of Vico, especially in *Il Diritto Universale*. The following, from A. R. Caponigri's discussion, is sufficient to show the similarity:

The task which confronts practical juris-
prudence is the interpretation of a law which
is offered to it as authoritative, as "certum"
in Vico's term, as embodying immediately
the concrete actuality of the law. The
intention of the law, however, is universal;
this intention embraces a class of instances
which fall under actual adjudication, even
though these instances, in all their particu-
larity, irreducible novelty and uniqueness,
could not have been foreseen or specifically
intended in the law. ... This universal intention of the law itself cannot be sustained
wholly by the law's certitude and authority;
on the contrary, it implies, within the intimate structure of the law, the presence of a
further element which is, in fact, in opposition to its certitude and authority and which
is the immediate vehicle of its intentional
universality. Thus, there emerges the concept of "verum" of the law, its truth, or
logical ground and ideal principle.[69]

The manner in which Vico transcends this
opposition of *verum* and *certum*, Gluckman's
"uncertainty" and "certainty", by presenting
them as the "dialectical moments of one con-
tinuous and dynamic process" so that their
"opposition is not abstract, but immanent to
the concreteness of this process", need not
concern us. What is important is that the recognition of the similarity of interest here involves
a view of social life and social analysis which

can have no place for models derived from natural science. Not only in the judicial process among the Barotse, but in the social process in which we live, the *verum* corresponds to what Cassirer called the forces which conserve—to language, institutions and beliefs, all that in our life which submits the individual to the social. But the *certum* corresponds to human experience at any given moment of what is, to particular decisions and actions, to particular events, to all in the total social process which is individual in that wide sense in which I have used that word here. The *verum* gives shape and meaning to what actually happens in time, the *certum* is the force and life of the *verum*.

Vico characterized his philosopher and his philologist as Plato and Tacitus. The first describes ideal man and the second man as he really is. His business, and the business of the social anthropologist, is not to participate in this debate by taking sides, but to recognize in social life the complementarity of the two. In this way the atemporal ideal is related to life, which is in time, and a model of society emerges as a dynamic system of thought-and-action.

Certainly no modern anthropologist would consciously attempt to separate thought from action in the society he studies. But the understanding he communicates is better to the extent that he departs from the conventional sociological view that the individual is irrelevant. Except in rare instances he has not developed the language in which to conceptualize these departures. An account, for example, of a particular form of family which described the ideal form which the people themselves conceive, and the ideal behaviour which the norms of society lay down, is not, even as a description, efficient. If, however, the anthropologist includes a description of particular individual families or people which, by their very individuality, diverge from these ideals, the divergences have to be accounted for by extraneous factors. They do not enter into the analysis nor can they if the at once static and organic model is applied. If, however, the particular family, or particular families, are seen as manifestations or local workings-out of the opposed forces making for aggregation on the one side and individualization on the other, a picture emerges which is true in the sense that it embraces more of what actually occurs, takes account of change and disengages a set of relations, however simple, which make possible a comparison, however elementary, with familiar forms in the same and in other societies.

As might be expected, the failure of the functionalist view comes out most clearly where we are faced with situations of upheaval and radical change. Several anthropologists in the last few years have paid attention to a phenomenon in the Pacific which goes under the general title of "Cargo Cult". This name has been given because one of the common features in the various localities where it has appeared is that the people destroy their goods and organize themselves in preparation for the imminent coming of the ancestors who will bring a lavish cargo for their children.[70] This cult, a blend of indigenous belief with Christian elements, has striking parallels elsewhere in the world and in the past. It is not ungenerous to say that at present the analysis, as opposed to the description of it, has hung fire and the terms by which it might be compared with similar movements are lacking. Evidently such a movement, violent, sudden and often short-lived, cannot be understood unless the pre-existing social order has been studied. Such studies are not lacking, since Polynesia and Melanesia have attracted several distinguished anthropologists. It is rather the case that the functionalist terms of their analyses, their preoccupation with groups and with relations between groups, left out of account the apprehension that those societies had of the individual; the social forms were not seen as, in a sense, coping with duration. These societies, however, were, even at the time they were studied, being subjected to a gathering flood of external experience which finally increased beyond the "stretch" of the indigenous categories that might render it meaningful. In Cassirer's terms, the balance between conservation and innovation was destroyed in favour of the latter. The social forms of communication appear inadequate. The society is as near to atomization into its component individuals as it could be. The last resort is a new stress upon the individual as that society conceives it, an emphasis upon history, upon individual possession by spirits, upon the individual inspired leader. We can say that what was individual and understressed in the normal rhythm of the society now becomes social and is stressed at the expense of forms which no longer render experience meaningful. This rapid sketch is offered only as an indication of a possible analysis, but it serves to show two things. Firstly, a prior analysis of the society conducted generally along the lines indicated would render these apparently hysterical outbursts more susceptible to analysis and secondly, the outbursts themselves could be compared in relational terms with similar phenomena elsewhere. The reader will no doubt have thought already of the increased number of possessions by sky-spirits reported by Professor Evans-Pritchard amongst the Nuer, "a response first to a challenge and then to disintegration". (See above, pp. 93-4). Faced with the threatening decay of the world in which they live, there occurs among the Nuer a proliferation of phenomena which before were rare and, as we have seen, regarded by the Nuer themselves as so individualistic as to be almost eccentric.

Social anthropology, then, if it is to develop must devise a language which enables us to conceive of society in duration. It is the play of society maintaining itself against, modifying itself to meet, the steady flow of new individuals

—whether people or events—which constitutes the object of our study: not that in society which makes for stability and communication only.

This language must also overcome the problems presented by simplicist notions of social determinism and of objectivity without rejecting what is profitable in these notions. Without some idea that society determines thought and action, the object of study ceases to exist. But if this notion is coupled with an idea of objectivity borrowed from natural science sociology destroys itself, for finally the observations of the sociologist himself are influenced not only by his national society but even by his class and intellectual milieu. Some have attempted to avoid the problem with the apparently commonsensical affirmation that it is our common humanity that provides the basis for our observations (and certainly, we study men). In these concluding sentences one can only reply that our common humanity makes us one, but society makes us many. Even that term "humanity" is variously defined and does not mean the same to the Brahman and to the Untouchable, to the White and the Black in South Africa. Social anthropology can transcend the observer and the observed without relinquishing the necessary postulate of some social determination, on the one hand, or relapsing into a hopeless and helpless moral relativism on the other.

Finally, social anthropology must justify its

claim to compare—not with the aim of arriving
at general and absolute classifications, but with
that of arriving at a more acute understanding
of particularities. Comparison in this sense is
concerned with similarities only to penetrate
more profoundly into the differences. The
comparison can only be conducted in terms of
relations, and not of items or isolated institutions; and this relational comparison begins
from the moment that the research worker
approaches his material. Social anthropology
compares from the outset, moving constantly
from the individual to the general and back to
a more refined understanding of the individual.
And before this can be done social anthropology
must liberate itself from the romantic conflict
of individual and society, and effect the union
of these opposites whose interaction is the
object of study.

> The being of one contrary is excluded by the
> being of the other; but the knowledge of one
> contrary is not excluded by knowledge of the
> other; indeed it is helped by it. So the
> qualities of opposites are not opposite in so
> far as they are entertained by the soul.[71]

NOTES

1. See E. E. Evans-Pritchard, *Social Anthropology*, London, Cohen and West, 1954; Raymond Firth, *Human Types*, revised ed., London, Nelson, 1956; S. F. Nadel, *The Foundations of Social Anthropology*, London, Cohen and West, 1951. R. G. Lienhardt's *Social Anthropology*, Oxford, 1964, J. H. M. Beattie's *Other Cultures*, London, 1964, and Lucy Mair's *An Introduction to Social Anthropology*, Oxford, 1965, appeared after the first edition of the present work.

2. Peter Winch, *The Idea of a Social Science and its Relation to Philosophy*, London, Routledge and Kegan Paul, 1958, p. 43.

3. *The New Science of Giambattista Vico*, trans. Bergin and Fisch (1744 edition), New York, Cornell University Press, 1948, pp. 56-7.

4. Beatrice Webb, *My Apprenticeship*, London, Longmans, 1926, p. xii.

5. The passage is included in *Social Contract: Essays by Locke, Hume and Rousseau*, ed. Sir Ernest Barker, Oxford University Press, 1946, p. 229.

6. Adam Ferguson, *An Essay in the History of Civil Society*, 1767, p. 12.

7. Ferguson, p. 25.

8. *The Spirit of the Laws*, by Baron de Montesquieu, trans. Nugent, New York, Hafner, 1949, preface, p. lxviii.

9. Émile Durkheim, *Montesquieu et Rousseau, précurseurs de la sociologie*, Paris, Rivière et Cie, 1953, p. 113.

10. George Henry Lewes, *The History of Philosophy from Thales to Comte*, 3rd ed., London, Longmans, 1867, p. 633.

11. Lewes, p. 608.

12. Francis Bacon, *The Advancement of Learning*, ed. W. A. Wright, 5th ed., Oxford, Clarendon Press, 1926, p. 97.

12a. There was not an "unimpeded march of science". For the co-existence of observed fact and pure fantasy about non-European societies see the excellent work of Margaret T. Hodgen, *Early Anthropology in the Sixteenth and Seventeenth Centuries*, Oxford, 1964.

13. K. R. H. Mackenzie in the *Popular Magazine of Anthropology*, London, vol. 1 (1866), p. 67.

14. T. Bendyshe, in *Memoirs of the Anthropological Society of London*, vol. 1 (1865).

15. Translated as *Introduction to Anthropology*, ed. J. Frederick Collingwood, London, 1863.

16. Charles Darwin, *The Descent of Man and Selection in Relation to Sex*, London, Murray, 1871.

17. Harold Peake and Herbert John Fleure, *Apes and Men*, Oxford, 1927 (*Corridors of Time*, vol. i), preface. Ten years later these authors recognized, in their ninth volume, *The Law and the Prophets*, the importance of Gräbner's "doctrines of the Diffusion of Culture".

18. Herbert Spencer, *The Study of Sociology*, London, Kegan Paul, Trench & Co., 1873, pp. 49, 50.

19. Spencer, p. 330.

20. Lewes, p. 610.

21. For a good account of the development in Durkheim's thought not taken into account here, see Talcott Parsons, *The Structure of Social Action*, Illinois, Free Press, 1949, pp. 301–460.

22. Émile Durkheim, "Individual and Collective Representations", in *Sociology and Philosophy*, trans. Pocock, London, Cohen and West, 1953.

23. Leibnitz, *Philosophical Writings*, London, Dent, 1934 (Everyman's Library), p. 143.

24. Leibnitz, p. 173.

25. Lewes, p. 610.

26. Macaulay, in the *Edinburgh Review* of June 1829 (in *Miscellaneous Writings of Lord Macaulay*, London, Routledge, 1893).

27. Durkheim, *Sociology and Philosophy*, p. 34.

28. My translation and italics. See *The Rules of Sociological Method*, trans. Solovay and Mueller, Illinois, Free Press, 1938, p. xliii.

29. C. Renouvier, *Essais de critique générale* (1854–64), vol. 1, p. 10.

30. *Année sociologique*, vol. 2 (1897–8), p. v.

31. Bronislaw Malinowski, *Argonauts of the Western Pacific*, London, Routledge, 1922, pp. 6–7.

32. Bronislaw Malinowski, "Anthropology", in *Encyclopaedia Britannica*, 13th ed.

33. A. R. Radcliffe-Brown, *The Andaman Islanders*, reprinted with additions, Cambridge University Press, 1933.

34. Radcliffe-Brown, p. vii.

35. Radcliffe-Brown, p. x.

36. Radcliffe-Brown, p. ix.

37. Radcliffe-Brown, *Andaman Islanders*, p. 401.

38. Radcliffe-Brown, *Andaman Islanders*, p. 403.

39. Durkheim, *Sociology and Philosophy*, p. 31.

40. See L. Dumont, in *Contributions to Indian Sociology*, The Hague, Mouton, vol. i (1957), p. 11.

41. A. R. Radcliffe-Brown, *Structure and Function in Primitive Society*, London, Cohen and West, 1952, ch. viii.

42. Melville J. Herskovits, *Man and His Works*, New York, Knopf, 1948, p. 29.

43. Talcott Parsons, p. 39.

44. E. E. Evans-Pritchard, *The Nuer*, Oxford, Clarendon Press, 1940, p. 266.

45. Evans-Pritchard, *The Nuer*, p. 136.

46. Evans-Pritchard, *The Nuer*, p. 16.

47. See the introduction to Marcel Mauss, *Sociologie et anthropologie*, Paris, Presses Universitaires, 1950, p. xlvii.

48. Ferguson, p. 31.

49. E. E. Evans-Pritchard, "Social Anthropology; Past and Present" (The Marett Lecture, 1950), published in *Man*, vol. 49 (1950), p. 118.

50. Max Gluckman, *Custom and Conflict in Africa*, Oxford, Blackwell, 1955, p. 2.

51. Lévi-Strauss, *Anthropologie structurale*, p. 306.

52. Lévi-Strauss, p. 307.

53. Lévi-Strauss, p. 309.

54. Introduction to Mauss, *Sociologie et anthropologie*, p. xlv.

55. R. G. Lienhardt, "The Shilluk of the Upper Nile", in *African Worlds*, ed. Daryll Forde, Oxford University Press, 1954; E. E. Evans-Pritchard, *The Political System of the Anuak of the Anglo-Egyptian Sudan*, London, 1940 (London School of Economics' Monographs on Social Anthropology, no. 4).

56. E. E. Evans-Pritchard, *Nuer Religion*, Oxford, Clarendon Press, 1956, p. 304.

57. Evans-Pritchard, *Nuer Religion*, p. 310.

58. Evans-Pritchard, *The Nuer*, p. 189.

59. *Nuer Religion*, p. 310.

60. Radcliffe-Brown, *Method in Social Anthropology*, p. 128.

61. *Method in Social Anthropology*, p. 128.

62. Ernst Cassirer, *An Essay on Man*, Yale University Press, 1944, p. 224.

63. Cassirer, p. 225.

64. Cf. Mircea Eliade, *The Myth of the Eternal Return*, trans. Trask, London, Routledge and Kegan Paul, 1955.

65. Max Gluckman, *The Judicial Process Among the Barotse of Northern Rhodesia*, Manchester, Manchester University Press, pp. 159–60.

66. Gluckman, *Judicial Process*, p. 160.

67. Gluckman, *Judicial Process*, p. 292.

68. Gluckman, *Judicial Process*, pp. 294–5.

69. Cf. A. R. Caponigri, *Time and Idea: The Theory of History in Giambattista Vico*, London, Routledge and Kegan Paul, 1953, p. 37.

70. For a general account of these movements see Kenelm Burridge, *New Heaven, New Earth*, Oxford, 1969, and Vittorio Lanternari, *The Religions of the Oppressed*, trans. Sergio, New York, 1963. For particular studies see Peter Worsley, *The Trumpet Shall Sound*, London, 1957, Kenelm Burridge, *Mambu, A Melanesian Millennium*, London, 1960, *Tangu Traditions*, Oxford, 1969, Peter Lawrence, *Road Belong Cargo*, London, 1964.

71. Aquinas, *In Metaphysicam Aristotelis Commentaria*, vii, 6. Cited by the late Victor White, O.P., in "Kinds of Opposites", in *Studien zur Analytischen Psychologie C. G. Jungs, Festschrift zum 80. Geburtstag, C. G. Jungs*, Zürich, Rascher Verlag 1955.